Winter Notes on Summer Impressions

Winter Notes on Summer Impressions

FYODOR DOSTOYEVSKY

Translated and introduced by
Kyril FitzLyon

Quartet Books
London   Melbourne   New York

This edition first published by
Quartet Books Limited 1985
A member of the Namara Group
27/29 Goodge Street, London W1P 1FD

The first edition was published under the title
Summer Impressions by John Calder 1955

British Library Cataloguing in Publication Data

Dostoyevsky, F.M.
Winter notes on summer impressions.
1. Europe—Description and travel—1800–1918
  I. Title   II.   Zimniye zametkio letnikh
      vpechatleniykh. *English*
      914'.04286   D919

ISBN 0–7043–2542–X

Typset by MC Typeset, Chatham, Kent
Printed and bound in Great Britain

Preface to this edition

When the first edition of this translation (with the title shortened to *Summer Impressions*) came out precisely thirty years ago, Dostoyevsky's *Winter Notes on Summer Impressions* had never been rendered into English before. I do not know whether another translation has appeared since then, but I do not think it has: certainly I have not been able to find it in the British Library Catalogue. By now my translation has been out of print for a number of years, which is probably why the author of the most recent study of Dostoyevsky in this country, was misled into assuring his readers that *Winter Notes* had never been translated into English at any time – a sad comment on the success of my efforts in that direction, but sadder still the fact that to most admirers of Dostoyevsky in the English-speaking world the work has remained totally unknown. And yet the history of the origin and development of some of Dostoyevsky's most cherished ideas, and of his attitude to Russia and the West cannot be either properly traced or even perhaps fully understood without reference to his *Winter Notes*. That little essay, as I have tried to show in my Introduction, has an importance out of all proportion to its modest size.

My translation is now being republished in the hope, if not the conviction, that Dostoyevskian studies in Great Britain have sufficiently progressed in the last thirty years for *Winter Notes* to be appreciated by many more readers than was the case a generation ago.

For the present edition I have somewhat expanded the Introduction while cutting out what now seems to me unnecessary comment and made some stylistic alterations, but left the main body of it intact. I have likewise introduced a few changes and additions to the comments that accompany the text of the translation. Translators are seldom entirely satisfied with the results of their work. Being no exception to this general rule, I could not refrain from introducing what I consider to be improvements in my translation. However, I have restricted myself to the barest minimum and the translation has remained substantially the same.

My rendering of, and changes in, the transliteration of Russian names (Dostoyevsky instead of Dostoievsky, Belinsky for Belinski, etc.) reflect my own wavering attitude to the matter and, perhaps, a fundamental, if unjustified, lack of interest in it. Certainly 'ye' as in 'yet' is, in English, a more familiar rendering of that sound than 'ie'. The '-sky' ending for Russian names is phonetically less correct than '-ski', but it has become traditional for them and distinguishes them from Polish names. Of course, the combination of the two ('-skiy') represents the most accurate rendering, but it is too pedantic for use outside a learned journal. Potemkin (recalling battleships to cinema fans and villages to amateurs of historical legends) would, I think, become unrecognizable to most readers in the phonetically more correct guise of 'Potyomkin' ('yo' as in 'yonder'). I have, therefore, left it without change.

K.F.

INTRODUCTION

I

IT IS USUAL to divide Dostoyevsky's literary activity into two distinct periods. The first opens with the publication in 1846 of a somewhat sentimental novel, *Poor Folk*, which brought him immediate literary renown, popular esteem and the enthusiastic blessing of the great critic Belinsky. It closes with what in effect are his reminiscences of life as a political convict (*The House of the Dead*), serialized in 1861–2 in his newly founded periodical *Vremya (Time)*. The second period, we are invariably told, is ushered in in 1864, with that oddly strident confession of personal guilt and inadequacy, entitled <u>Notes from Underground</u>, and finishes with the *Pushkin Commemoration Address* delivered a few months before his death.

To state that Dostoyevsky's writings fall into two fairly definite periods is, of course, to state the obvious; the author's attitude to the world, his choice of subject matter and his treatment of plot undergo in the '60s of the last century profound change. His earlier novels aim mainly at the entertainment of the reader; undeterred by considerations of verisimilitude or psychological insight, they lack the later Dostoyevskian eagerness <u>to reconcile the actions</u> <u>of men with their consciences,</u> conceived in terms of spiritual anguish.

The opening of the second and more characteristic phase of Dostoyevsky's literary activity was introduced not, it seems to me, by *Notes from Underground*, but in the previous year, by a short work – no more than an essay – very little commented on hitherto. The significance of the essay, to which he gave the name *Winter Notes on Summer Impressions*, is quite disproportionate to its length for the light it throws on the origin and development of Dostoyevsky's most cherished ideas.

Dostoyevsky, fresh from his first contact with Western Europe (which included a week in London and three in Paris), published in his periodical his impressions of that new and alien world using them as a peg on which to hang a remarkable number of the ideas which henceforth entered in varying degrees into everything he wrote, often expressed in phrases lifted textually from the present book. It is hardly an exaggeration to say that he never again wrote anything which contained so many of his thoughts on so many subjects in so few pages. It was as if, on the threshold of an entirely new epoch in his writing, he had decided to present his readers with a profession of faith and a synopsis of his ideas. In fact, *Winter Notes on Summer Impressions*, far from deserving their Cinderella-like treatment, ought to be regarded as a chrysalis out of which developed such masterpieces as *The Devils, Crime and Punishment* and *The Brothers Karamazov*, as well as the *Journal of an Author* and the figures of Father Zosima and the Grand Inquisitor. Even the *Pushkin Commemoration Address*, which was probably received with greater immediate acclamation than anything Dostoyevsky had ever written, contains little that is not adumbrated in the present book.

The neglect from which *Winter Notes* have suffered at the hands of literary critics is due to a variety of reasons. One of them, no doubt, is that it is generally regarded as a piece of journalistic *reportage* with no bearing on the great novels on which Dostoyevsky's reputation rests, rather than as a link in his whole system of thought. Another reason may be the style of writing Dostoyevsky adopted for his *Winter Notes* in which repetitiveness, excessive colloquialism, forced breeziness and waggish humour tend to predominate to the irritation of the reader. The reader must make up his mind to disregard these things. If he does, he will be amply rewarded.

II

THE CENTRE of Dostoyevsky's ideas harbours a vision of the world as a moral and spiritual unity, a 'brotherly fellowship', which must 'exist in nature', but cannot be artificially created (as both *Winter Notes* and Father Zosima phrase it) and which expects, but most definitely does not demand, of its members a total responsibility for each other and for the community as a whole. It is a unity which makes each one of us into a link in the infinite chain of causation and which, though it may relieve each individual member of the human race of total responsibility and therefore total guilt, yet thrusts upon each of us the burden of a world conscience. It is this theme which Dostoyevsky later expanded into an analytical novel (*Crime and Punishment*) and which later still he made both his Grand Inquisitor and Father Zosima (*The Brothers Karamazov*) develop each in his own way.

The fundamental tragedy of men, according to Dostoyevsky, comes from two kinds of actions: actions that shatter world unity (and every crime committed against one's fellow men is an attempt to shatter it, as Raskolnikov in *Crime and Punishment* finds out to his cost) and actions which attempt to attain a synthetic unity by artificial means. The latter he considers particularly dangerous; for men, consciously or subconsciously aware of the dangers of 'isolation', all clamour for unity, and, in default of genuine brotherhood, are all too eager to accept a counterfeit model in the shape of socialism or the Catholic Church, which can offer nothing but the brotherhood of an 'ant-hill'. But, says Dostoyevsky, both in his *Winter Notes on Summer Impressions* and in his capacity of Grand Inquisitor (*The Brothers Karamazov*), even this men will gladly accept, for the alternative to an ant-hill is a struggle of all against all, ending in 'cannibalism', when men will devour each other. Catholicism and socialism Dostoyevsky regarded as being basically the same, both of them ultimately emanations of the Roman Imperial idea, which insisted on a purely mechanical, external unification of men, in the hope (at least on the part of the Catholic Church) that such a unification would in time give birth to true spiritual fellowship.[1] This, thought Dostoyevsky, was putting the cart before the horse, a mistake never committed by the Orthodox Church. In his interpretation, the Orthodox Church expected unity to come of itself, spontaneously and with no assistance from external human agencies; and when it came, true brotherhood would be established with no need for any rules or constitutions.

In essence, of course, this is merely the Slavophil version of Russian anarchism, which was conceived as a blend of Freedom and Love, the former without the latter leading to anarchy, as distinct from anarchism, or to 'isolation' in the Dostoyevskian sense, the latter without the former not, in fact, able to exist. From Dostoyevsky's point of view, the importance of this attitude on the part of the Orthodox Church was that the Church, after being adopted by the Russian people, made Russia for ever

---

[1] The identity of Catholicism and socialism is an idea which clearly had not yet taken its final shape in Dostoyevsky's mind at the time of writing *Winter Notes*. He was convinced then that 'socialism [was] possible anywhere but in France'. Yet, later on, in his *Journal*, he argues that France is socialist already *because* she has a Catholic tradition, however much she may repudiate that tradition.

different from the West. And it is just because the West is regarded by him as the true abode of 'individualist isolation' in contrast to Russia's strivings after a spiritual synthesis of the community, that the theme of Europe and her civilization recurs so frequently in Dostoyevsky's writings after his return to Russia.

His analysis of Western Europe, first outlined in *Winter Notes* and thereafter relentlessly pursued through the pages of most of his books and particularly of his *Journal*, presents a strange amalgam of Slavophil prejudice and Fourierist ideals, of religious utopianism and historical materialism, of traditionalist concepts expressed in terms reminiscent of the Communist Manifesto. His earlier enthusiasm for Fourier – the cause, indeed, of his sojourn in the 'House of the Dead' – and his acute awareness of those social and economic forces that lie at the bottom of our cultural edifice, lead him to give certain historical events an interpretation rendered familiar to us by Marxist writings. Thus he regards the French Revolution as a mere sham, benefiting no one but the middle-classes, the bourgeoisie, at once the emanation and the creator of capitalism, whom the Revolution enabled to obtain a firm grip on the proletariat in order to exploit it. The hollowness of the Revolution, he says significantly enough in his *Journal*, was exposed by the execution of Babeuf, the apostle of early communism.

This attitude colours the whole of his approach to France with which most of the present book is concerned. Like Marx, he refuses to see in the Revolution's and, later, the Republic's, slogan – Liberty, Equality, Fraternity – anything but a piece of bourgeois hypocrisy, a gigantic bluff; considers, like Marx, that there can be no real freedom in Western Europe without the transference of economic power to the proletariat; like Marx, believes that proletarians are bound to unite – 'form their own heap' – in defence of their own interests without the fraudulent pretence of speaking for humanity as a whole; has the true Marxist (and Slavophil) contempt for Western liberalism and for all forms of parliamentary government, and, like Marx again, sees in the whole network of European social policy and behaviour nothing but the bourgeoisie's frantic attempt to retain the status quo. But the proletariat, he says, is knocking at the door and one day will force it open. Repudiated by the bourgeoisie and kept away from this world's goods it is ready to join in the class struggle and eager to repudiate the repudiators.

It is obviously a theme that haunted Dostoyevsky, for having dealt with it in some detail in his *Winter Notes*, he returned to it and repeated it with exasperating frequency in his *Journal* many years later. No doubt his insistence on the dire fate awaiting the Western capitalist world, though often expressed in quasi-Marxist terms, was due to highly un-Marxist causes. It was due, in fact, to the wishful thinking of a Russian nationalist obsessed by the fear of Western supremacy, and suffering, like so many Russians, from an acute inferiority complex vis-à-vis the West.

As a result Dostoyevsky fails to apply his semi-Marxist analysis to his own country, but, on the contrary, claims that no proletarian revolution is possible in Russia for the simple reason that the Russian proletariat is not only contented but is becoming increasingly so. He does, however, in his *Winter Notes* and later in his other works, raise one point – one of the most interesting in the present book because touching upon perhaps the most fateful of all Russian nineteenth-century weaknesses, more objectionable in Dostoyevsky's view than some of the worst excesses of serfdom and more destabilizing in its effect than inequalities of income: the inequalities of culture, which split the country in two and resulted in the loss of contact between the educated classes and the peasantry. It was, he felt, this loss of contact which led to lack of understanding on both sides, to an attitude of supercilious superiority or guilty fawning on the part of the educated classes and a half-sullen, half-contemptuous withdrawal into their own community by the peasants, to the treatment of the latter by the former as if, to quote Dostoyevsky, they were 'enemy tribes'; it led to the rootlessness of the intelligentsia, it led to the Slavophil movement which had Dostoyevsky's full and active sympathy, but whose ridiculous sides (like the wearing of bogus national dress to placate the 'enemy tribes') he was quick to perceive, and it led to the phenomenon of 'Westernizing expatriates' – Russians who felt more at home in Western Europe than they did in their own country where they found no congenial occupation for themselves, stayed out of Russia as much as they could and were a constant butt for Dostoyevsky's rather heavy-handed sarcasm. In the following century it may have been a contributary cause of the Russian Revolution.

III

THE MARQUIS DE CUSTINE whose very brief stay in Russia preceded Dostoyevsky's visit to Paris by a whole genera-tion and resulted in a book perhaps more often quoted than read, was shocked by the lack of freedom in Russia, the ubiquity of police informers, the arbitrariness of government and the slavish adulation of the Emperor. He ascribed it all either expressly or by implication to national character as well as to the country's remoteness from the civilizing influence of Western Europe in general and of France in particular. When a quarter of a century later, in the summer of 1862, Dostoyevsky came to Paris, he too, was shocked, and, what shocked him, so he confesses or implies in his *Winter Notes*, was lack of freedom in France, the ubiquity of police informers, the arbitrariness of government and the slavish adulation of the Emperor. He ascribes it all to national character which produced the French bourgeois with his servile mentality.

The impact made on Dostoyevsky by this country was strikingly different. For the moment (for he vacillated in this) he despised the French, and Paris, he wrote to a friend, bored him to death. But London overwhelmed him. True, the picture he draws of it and of the British social scene is somehow reminiscent of Gustave Doré's illustrations for Dante's *Inferno*, and he is driven to describe it in apocalyptic terms, but at least there is no room in it for the meanness and pettiness which he found across the Channel. It is curious too, that his judgement of the two countries completely reverses the more usual view, accepted as axiomatic by the world at large. It is France, not England, in his estimation, that is a nation of shopkeepers, and it is France that is hypocritical when it comes to moral standards, for she tries to slur over and, if possible, hide certain distasteful facts of life such, for instance, as irregularity of sexual behaviour, commercial dishonesty and the presence of poverty in the midst of plenty. Dostoyevsky's England has her share of social vices, but they are there for everyone to see: no attempt is made to conceal them. In fact, if France's outstanding trait is hypocrisy, England's is pride.

It is clear, of course, that Dostoyevsky did not form his impressions of England unaided. A week's stay in London could not have either supplied him with the necessary material or given him a sufficient insight into the British character, particularly as he knew no English. (He admits to his ignorance of the language in one passage of the present book, yet in another claims to base certain of his conclusions on English newspaper reports.) The only man Dostoyevsky is known to have visited in England was Alexander Herzen, the exiled Russian journalist of radical views, a sparkling personality and a brilliant talker, whose opinion of the Russian government Dostoyevsky did not share, but whose views of the English character and customs he evidently found congenial. It is Herzen's views, therefore, that, more likely than not, form the basis of Dostoyevsky's analysis of the English character and of life in this country.

But quite apart from his influence on Dostoyevsky's views about this country, Herzen is responsible for much of the contents of *Winter Notes* as well as for the form in which they were cast; the perusal of his *Letters from France and Italy* makes this abundantly clear. For these *Letters* have suggested to Dostoyevsky many of his reflections on Russia and his few remarks on Germany, and provided him with some of the more biting images which he used in order to illustrate his comments on the French contemporary social scene and the bourgeois' mentality and habits.

In general, Dostoyevsky was readily influenced by contemporary thinkers, and the game of tracing his ideas back to their original sources is not hard to play. Thus, Petrashevsky inspired him with his early enthusiasm for Fourier, which, for all his later scoffing, continued to colour his vision; his concept of universality as the most typical attribute of the Russian character was probably first suggested to him by Belinsky who himself owed it to Odoyevsky; his notion of true brotherhood, realizable through a spontaneous integration of society and the individual, is similar to Constantine Aksakov's and to Khomyakov's; Samarin is partly responsible for his view of the Orthodox Church as the synthesis of the Roman Catholic principle of unity and the Protestant principle of freedom; the two alternatives of 'ant-hill' and 'cannibal-ism' are derived from Herzen; so is much of the language he uses to express his social and political philosophy, though there Petrashevsky's contribution looms large indeed; while, in so far as it differs from Herzen's, his view of the West – its individualism, materialism and impending calamitous decline – and of Russia's special place in the comity of nations and almost in the Universe – her self-contained civilization and messianic destiny – can be found in all essentials in early Slavophil literature.

Dostoyevsky's failure entirely to fuse all these disparate elements into one properly integrated whole till very late in life, resulted in an ambivalence of attitude to the problems of his day which would have been fatal to a lesser man. That it did not prove fatal is due to a combination of qualities which include sincerity, psychological insight and immense literary gifts.

CHAPTER I

INSTEAD OF A PREFACE

FOR MONTHS NOW, my friends, you have been urging me to give you a description of my impressions while travelling in foreign lands, never suspecting that you are thereby placing me in a quandary. What shall I tell you? What shall I say that is new, that has not been told before? Who of us Russians (those, at least, that read periodicals) does not know Europe twice as well as he knows Russia? I have put down 'twice' merely out of politeness. I should probably have said 'ten times better'. Besides apart from these general considerations you are well aware that I, of all people, have nothing to tell and least of all can I give a methodical account of anything, because there was no method in my sight-seeing, and even when I did see anything I did not have time to examine it very closely. I visited Berlin, Dresden, Wiesbaden, Baden-Baden, Cologne, Paris, London, Lucerne, Geneva, Genoa, Florence, Milan, Venice, Vienna and a few other places (to which I went twice), and the whole tour took me precisely two and a half months! Now, I ask you, is it possible to see anything thoroughly while travelling over so many roads in the course of two and a half months?

You will remember that I composed my itinerary while still in St Petersburg. I had never been abroad, but I longed to go there even as a small child, when, still unable to read, I listened agape, enthralled and terror-struck in turn, to my parents' bed-time reading of Mrs Radcliffe's novels

1

which put me in a fever and kept me awake at night. When at last I wrenched myself away from my preoccupations and went abroad I was forty years of age and, naturally enough, I was not content with seeing as much as possible, I wanted to see everything – yes, everything – despite the time limit. Besides, I was quite incapable of coolly choosing places to visit. Heavens, how much I expected from my tour! 'It doesn't matter if I don't look at things in great detail,' I thought. 'I shall, at least have seen everything and been everywhere, and all I have seen will have fused itself into one whole and made up a kind of general panorama. I shall, at one fell swoop, have had a bird's eye view of the entire "land of holy miracles" like the Promised Land from the mountain – in perspective.[1] In fact, I shall experience a new, wonderful and mighty impression.' After all, what do I regret most now, sitting at home and recalling my summer time wanderings? Not that I saw nothing in great detail, but that although I have been almost everywhere, I have not, for example, been in Rome. And in Rome I might, perhaps, have missed the Pope. . . . In fact, I was overwhelmed by an unquenchable thirst for something new, for a constant change of place, for general, synthetic, panoramic, perspective impress-ions.

Now what do you expect from me after such a confession? What shall I tell you? What shall I depict? A panorama? A perspective? A bird's eye view of something? But you will probably be the first to tell me that I have flown too high. Besides, I consider myself to be a conscientious man, and I should not at all like to tell lies, or even travellers' tales. But even should I limit myself to depicting and describing the panoramic view, I could not fail to tell lies and not even because I am a traveller, but

[1]'Land of holy miracles' – name given to Western Europe by the Slavophil poet A. Khomyakov (1804–60) in his poem 'A Dream' (1834). *Tr. note.*

simply because in such circumstances as mine it is impossible not to lie. Reason it out for yourselves. Berlin, for instance, made a very sour impression on me and I stayed only twenty-four hours in it. But I know now that I have wronged Berlin, that I have no right to my assertion that it makes a sour impression. There is a dash of sweetness in it, at the very least. And what was the cause of that fatal mistake of mine? Simply the fact that though a sick man, suffering from an attack of liver, I sped along through rain and fog to Berlin for two whole days and nights and when I arrived after a sleepless journey, yellow, tired and broken, I noticed suddenly and at the very first glance that Berlin was incredibly like St Petersburg. The same monotonously straight streets, the same smells, the same. . . (but I cannot enumerate all the things they have in common)! Blow me, I thought to myself, it was really hardly worth while spending a back-breaking forty-eight hours in a railway carriage only to see the replica of what I had just left. I did not even like the lime-trees, to preserve which a Berliner will sacrifice all he holds most dear, even his constitution; and what can be dearer to a Berliner than his constitution? Besides, all Berliners, all of them without exception, looked so German that (oh, horror!) without so much as an attempt to see Kaulbach's frescoes I slipped away to Dresden as fast as I could, deeply convinced in my heart of hearts that it needed a special knack to get used to a German and that at first he was very difficult to bear in large masses.

In Dresden I was unfair even to German women. I decided immediately I stepped out into the street, that no sight was more horrible than a typical Dresden woman, and that even Vsevolod Krestovsky, that poet of love and the most inveterately gay of all Russian poets, might despair and come to doubt his vocation.[1] Of course I felt

[1] V. Krestovsky (1840–95) a very minor poetaster, and third-rate novelist. *Tr. note.*

the very same minute that I was talking nonsense and that under no circumstances whatever could he possibly come to doubt his vocation. A couple of hours later I realized what it was: back in my hotel bedroom I put out my tongue in front of a mirror and had to confess that my opinion of the ladies of Dresden was in the highest degree slanderous. My tongue was yellow and unpleasant. . . 'Can it really be true,' thought I, 'that man, that lord of creation, is so dependent on his own liver? How low!'

With these comforting thoughts I went off to Cologne. I admit to having expected a lot from the Cathedral of which I reverently made drawings in my youth when I studied architecture. On my way back through Cologne a month later, when I saw the Cathedral a second time on my return from Paris, I almost 'asked its forgiveness on my knees' for not having fully grasped its beauty, just like Karamzin fell on his knees in front of a Rhine water-fall.[1] But all the same, that first time I did not like the Cathedral at all; it seemed to me to be nothing but a piece of lace, lace and lace again, a bit of fancy goods, something like a paper-weight, some 500 feet high.

'Not very majestic,' I decided, just as our grandfathers concluded about Pushkin: 'His writings are too light,' they used to say, 'not enough of the lofty style in them.'

I suspect that this first opinion of mine was influenced by two circumstances, the first of them being eau-de-Cologne. Jean-Maria-Farina is situated next to the Cathedral, and no matter at which hotel you stay, whatever your mood, however hard you may be trying to hide from your enemies and particularly from Jean-Maria-Farina, his

[1]N. Karamzin (1766–1826) – historian, poet and novelist, strongly influenced by eighteenth-century British writers, such as Sterne and Richardson. His *Poor Liza* (1792), a lachrymose and sentimental little tale, had an enormous success and is generally considered to be the first Russian novel. The sentence quoted in this context comes out of his Swiss letters (dated 14 August 1789). *Tr. note.*

clients are sure to find you, and then it is the case of 'eau-de-Cologne ou la vie' – one of the two, there is no other choice. I cannot assert too definitely that these are the very words people shout: 'eau-de-Cologne ou la vie', but who knows, perhaps they are? I remember at that time I kept imagining I could hear them.

The second circumstance which irritated me and made me unfair in my judgments was the new Cologne bridge. The bridge is excellent, of course, and the town is justly proud of it, but I thought it was too proud of it. Naturally this made me angry. Besides the collector of pennies at the entrance to the marvellous bridge should not have made me pay that reasonable tax with an air of fining me for some misdemeanour of which I myself was not aware. I don't know, but it struck me that the German was trying to bully me. 'He has probably guessed,' I thought, 'that I am a foreigner, and a Russian at that.' Anyway, his eyes almost as good as said: 'You see our bridge, you miserable Russian? Well, you are a mere worm in comparison with our bridge and with every Cherman man because you haven't got a bridge like that.' You must agree this is enough to make one take offence. The German never said it, of course, and never even harboured it in his thoughts perhaps, but it does not matter. I was so convinced that that was just what he wanted to say, that I completely lost my temper. 'Damn it all,' I thought, 'we have something to be proud of too, the samovar for instance. . . We've got magazines. . . We make first-class things. . . We have. . .' In short, I lost my temper, and, after buying a bottle of eau-de-Cologne which I could not avoid, I immediately rushed off to Paris in the hope that the French would be a great deal nicer and more entertaining.

Now you reason it out for yourselves: if only I had made an effort and stayed a week in Berlin instead of one day, the same in Dresden and say about three days, or two at the very least, in Cologne, I should most probably have

5

had another or even a third glimpse of the same things, but with a different eye and should have obtained a more favourable impression of them. Even a ray of sunshine, just an ordinary ray of sunshine, would have had a lot to do with it; if only the sun had shone over the Cathedral as it in fact did shine when I arrived in the city of Cologne for the second time, the whole building would have appeared to me in its true light and not as it did that bleak and even somewhat rainy morning, fit only to provoke an outburst of wounded patriotism. It by no means follows, however, that patriotism is only born in bad weather.

And so you see, my friends, you cannot look at everything in two and a half months and never make a mistake, and I am unable to give you the most accurate information. I must willy-nilly be untruthful occasionally, and therefore. . .

But here you interrupt me. You tell me that this time you do not, in fact, want accurate information, that if need be you will find it in Reichard's guidebook, and that, on the contrary, it would not be at all a bad thing if travellers aimed not so much at absolute truth (which they are almost never able to attain) as at sincerity, if sometimes they were not afraid to reveal some personal impression or adventure, even of the kind that did not redound much to their credit, and if they did not look up well-known authorities in order to check up on their own conclusions. You tell me, in short, that all you want are my own impressions, provided they are sincere.

Ah! say I, so what you want is just gossip, light sketches, fleeting personal impressions. That certainly suits me and I shall immediately consult my diary. And I shall try to be as simple and frank as possible. I only ask you to bear in mind that I shall often be wrong in the things I write about. Not wrong about everything, of course. One cannot be wrong about such facts, for instance, as that the Cathedral of Notre Dame is in Paris and so is the Bal Mabille. The latter fact in particular has been so thoroughly recorded by all Russians writing about Paris that it is almost impossible to doubt it. Even *I* shall not perhaps make a mistake about this, though strictly speaking, I cannot guarantee even this. Now, for example, they say that it is impossible to go to Rome and not see St Peter's. But just think: I have been in London, but never saw St Paul's. Honestly, I did not. Never saw St Paul's Cathedral. True enough, there is quite a difference between St Peter's and St Paul's, but all the same, it is somehow hardly decent for a traveller not to have seen it. There's my first adventure for you, which does not redound much to my credit (that is to say, I did in fact see it perhaps, at a distance of some 500 yards, but I was in a hurry to get to Pentonville, did not bother and ignored it). But let us be more to the point. And do you know – I did not just travel about and enjoy a bird's-eye-view of things (enjoying a bird's-eye-view of things does not mean looking down on them. It is an architectural term, you know.) I stayed in Paris for a whole month less the eight days I spent in London. And so I shall now write something about Paris for you, because I have, after all, had a much better look at it than I had at St Paul's Cathedral or at the ladies of Dresden. Well, here goes.

Chapter II

IN A RAILWAY CARRIAGE

'FRENCHMEN ARE not rational and would consider themselves most unfortunate if they were.' This phrase was written by Fonvizin as far back as the last century, and, Heavens, how cheerfully he must have written it.[1] I bet the sheer joy of it warmed the cockles of his heart when he was thinking it up. and who knows, perhaps all of us coming after Fonvizin, three or four generations at a stretch, read it not without pleasure. All such phrases, which put foreigners in their place, contain, even if we come across them now, something irresistibly pleasant for us Russians. We keep this very secret, sometimes, even secret from ourselves. For there are in this certain overtones of revenge for an evil past. Maybe this is a bad feeling, but somehow I am convinced it exists in almost every one of us. Naturally enough, we kick up a fuss if we are suspected of it, and are not one bit insincere, and yet I should imagine Belinsky[2] himself was in this sense a

---

[1]Denis Fonvizin (1744–92) – 'the Father of Russian Comedy', author of *The Brigadier* (1766). The present quotation comes from Letter XLIV, written from Aachen on 29 September 1778, and addressed to General P. Panin. The rest of the sentence is as follows: '. . . for it would force them to think instead of enjoying themselves.' *Tr. note.*

[2]Vissarion Belinsky (1811–48) – the most famous of all Russian literary critics at a time when literary criticism performed also the function of social and political criticism. He was a radical and a 'Westerner' in his sympathies. *Tr. note.*

8

Slavophil. I remember about fifteen years ago, when I knew Belinsky, how reverently (sometimes even oddly so) all that set used to bow down and worship the West, mostly France that is. France was all the fashion then – this was in 'forty-six. And it is not that people adored such names as Georges Sand, Proudhon, etc. and felt respect for those of Louis Blanc, Ledru-Rollin and others. Oh no! People thought highly even of little pip-squeaks, bearing the most wretched names, who simply collapsed when they were put on their mettle later on. Even those were expected to perform great deeds in the future service to humanity. Some of them were talked about in a special reverent whisper. . . And what do you think? In all my life I have never seen a man more passionately Russian than was Belinsky, though before him only Chaadayev perhaps spoke with such bold and sometimes blind indignation about much in our native land and apparently despised everything Russian.[1] There are certain reasons why I should remember and think of it now. But who knows, maybe Belinsky himself did not always consider that *mot* of Fonvizin's particularly scandalous. Surely there are moments when people fail to appreciate the most seemly and indeed legitimate tutelage. Oh, but for Heaven's sake, don't run away with the idea that to love one's country means to revile the foreigner or that I think it does. I don't think so at all and have no intention of thinking so, on the contrary even. . . Only it is a pity I have no time to explain myself somewhat more clearly.

By the way, please don't think that I have forgotten Paris and launched myself into Russian literature instead, or that I am writing an article of literary criticism. It's only because I have nothing else to do.

[1]Peter Chaadayev (1794–1856) – author of *Lettres Philosophiques*, in which the value of all Russian cultural achievements is vehemently denied, and Western Europe is proclaimed to be the only source of light. *Tr. note.*

My diary tells me that I am now sitting in a railway carriage and am getting ready to see Eydtkuhnen tomorrow, to receive, that is, my first impression of a foreign country, and my heart even misses a beat occasionally. Shall I really see Europe at last, I who have vainly dreamt of it for almost forty years, I who when still only sixteen, in dead earnest and like Nekrasov's Belopyatkin,[1] 'wished to flee to Switzerland', but did not flee and am now about to enter 'the land of holy miracles',[2] the land for which I have yearned so long and from which I expected so much, and in which I believed so implicitly.

'Good heavens,' I kept thinking as I sat in the railway carriage, 'how can we be called Russians? Are we really Russians in fact? Why does Europe make such a powerful and magic impression on all of us whoever we are? Why does it appeal to us so much?' I don't mean to those Russians who stay at home, those ordinary Russians whose name is Fifty Million, on whom we, all the one hundred thousand of us, look with disdain and whom our profound satirical journals make fun of, because they do not shave their beards. No, I mean our privileged and patented little group.

After all, everything, literally almost everything we can show which may be called progress, science, art, citizenship, humanity, everything, everything stems from there, from that land of holy miracles. The whole of our life, from earliest childhood, is shaped by the European mould. Could any one of us have withstood this influence, appeal, pressure? How is it that we have still not been finally metamorphosed into Europeans? And I think everyone will agree that we have not been metamorphosed – some with pleasure, others, of course, with fury because we have not yet *reached* metamorphosis. But that is

[1]Nikolai Nekrasov (1821–78) – Russian poet. Belopyatkin is the hero of one of his early poems. *Tr. note.*
[2]See note 1, page 2.

another matter. I am merely speaking about the fact that we have not been metamorphosed even after being subjected to such an overwhelming influence, and am at a loss to account for it. It could surely not have been our nannies and mammies that have preserved us from metamorphosis. It is sad and absurd, really, to think that but for Arina Rodionovna, Pushkin's nurse, we should, perhaps, have had no Pushkin. That is nonsense, is it not? Of course it is. and what if in fact it is not nonsense? Many Russian children are now being brought up in France; what if another Pushkin has been taken there to be deprived from his cradle upwards both of an Arina Rodionovna and of Russian speech?

No one could have been more Russian than Pushkin. Though himself of gentle birth, he yet understood Pugachev and penetrated right into his innermost being at a time when nobody penetrated anywhere.[1] An aristocrat, he yet carried Belkin within his soul.[2] By the force of his artistry he renounced his class and in *Onegin* judged it with stern judgement from the standpoint of the nation as a whole.[3] He is a prophet and a forerunner.

Is there really a chemical bond between the human spirit and a man's native land which makes it impossible to break away from one's country and even if one does break away from it, makes one come back to it in the end? After all, Slavophilism did not fall in our midst straight out of the clear sky, and though it did afterwards become a Moscovite fad, the basis of this fad is considerably broader

[1]Pugachev – an eighteenth-century leader, of a peasant revolt, depicted by Pushkin in his history of the revolt and in a short novel *The Captain's Daughter*. Tr. note.
[2]In 1831 Pushkin published a collection of five short stories supposedly written by a retired officer of modest means 'the late Ivan Petrovich Belkin'. Tr. note.
[3]Onegin – the hero of Pushkin's most famous poem *Eugene Onegin* (1824–28). Tr. note.

than allowed for by Moscow's formula and lies possibly much deeper in some people's hearts than seems likely at first sight. In fact, even in Moscow this basis is perhaps broader than Moscow's own formula. It is at first so terribly difficult to express oneself clearly even to oneself.

Some ideas, though powerful and full of vitality, take over three generations fully to manifest themselves so that their final end does not resemble their beginnings in the very slightest. . .

Thus did all these idle thoughts assail me in my railway carriage on the way to Europe, partly in spite of myself and partly because I was bored and had nothing to do. To be frank, only those of us who have nothing to do have hitherto given thought to this sort of thing. Oh, how boring it is to sit idly in a railway carriage! In fact, just as boring as it is to live in Russia without having anything specific to do. You may be taken along and cared for, you may even be lulled to sleep sometimes, indeed your every wish may be anticipated, but you are bored, bored all the same, and precisely because you are being cared for and all you have to do is to sit and wait till you are brought to your destination. Honestly, one sometimes feels like jumping out of the carriage and running along by the side of the engine on one's own flat feet. The results may be worse, lack of practice may soon tire one out, but at least one would be using one's own legs and doing a job one has found oneself, and were the carriage to collide and turn somersaults one would not be sitting shut in and twirling one's thumbs and one would not be answerable for someone else's blunder. . .

What extraordinary ideas one gets when one has nothing to do!

In the meantime, night was drawing on. Lights were being lit in the carriages. I had a husband and wife sitting opposite me, elderly people, landowners and probably respectable. They were in a hurry to get to London for the

Exhibition, but only for a few days and they had left their family at home.[1] Sitting next to me on my right was a Russian who had been working in an office in London for the last ten years, who had come to St Petersburg on business for just a fortnight and who seemed to have lost all sense of longing for his native land. On my left sat a clean, pure-bred Englishman, intensely serious and with his red hair parted in the English way. Throughout the journey he never said a single word in any language to any of us; he read all day without lifting his head a book of that very small English print which only English people can tolerate and even praise for its convenience, and at precisely ten o'clock at night he took off his boots and put on slippers. He was probably used to doing this all his life and had no desire to change his habits even in a railway carriage.

Soon everyone was dozing; the whistling and knocking sounds of the train made one terribly sleepy. I sat and thought and thought and somehow – I do not know how – came to the conclusion that 'Frenchmen were not rational', which served as the beginning of this chapter. And, do you know, I am impelled by something or other, while we are making our way to Paris, to let you know of my carriage thoughts, just like that, for the sake of human sympathy: after all I was bored enough, sitting in that carriage, so you might as well be bored now. However, other readers should be protected, and I shall, therefore, deliberately include all these thoughts in one chapter which I shall call *superfluous*. It will bore you a little, but as it is superfluous other people can simply leave it out. The reader must be treated carefully and conscientiously, but friends can be dealt with a little more cavalierly.

Well, now. . .

[1]The reference is to the World Exhibition of 1862. Though historically not as famous as its predecessor, the Great Exhibition of 1851, it, in fact, exceeded it in extent, cost, attendance, and number of exhibitors. *Tr. note.*

Chapter III

WHICH IS QUITE SUPERFLUOUS

As a matter of fact, these were not thoughts, but a sort of contemplation, arbitrary notions, day-dreams even, 'of this and that, and nothing else'. To begin with, I made a mental jouney back into olden times and let my thoughts wander, particularly on the subject of the man who had made the above aphorism about the rationality of Frenchmen. It was, in fact, the aphorism that gave rise to these otherwise aimless thoughts. For his day that man held very progressive ideas. But though he did go about all his life bedecked in the dress of a French gentleman, powdered wig and a little sword to show his knightly descent (which was entirely foreign to us) and to defend his personal honour in Potemkin's waiting room, no sooner did he poke his nose abroad than the very name of Paris became anathema to him and he decided that 'Frenchmen were not rational' and that they would even consider it most unfortunate if they were.[1] By the way, you do not by any chance imagine, do you, that I mentioned the sword and the velvet coat as a reproach to Fonvizin? Because I certainly did not. He could not, after all, put on a Russian peasant coat, particularly at that time, when even now certain persons, in order *to be Russian* and merge with the people do not put on a peasant coat, but have instead

[1]Gregory Potemkin (1735–91): Russian general and statesman; one of the most powerful of Catherine II's favourites.

14

invented a ballet dress for themselves little different from the type worn in Russian national operas by the various Ouslads in love with their Ludmillas wearing kokoshniks.[1] At least, a French coat was nearer to the people's understanding of things: 'You can see he's a gentleman,' they would say. 'What else should a gentleman wear – a peasant's coat or something?'

I heard a short time ago that one modern landowner in order to merge with the people also took to wearing *Russian dress* and even going to village meetings in it; but the peasants as soon as they saw him coming would say to each other: 'What's this fellow in fancy dress barging in here for?' So that landowner had no success in merging with the people.

'I shall certainly not make any concessions,' a friend said to me. 'I certainly shan't – not me! I will make a point of not wearing a beard, and I'll go about in white tie and tails if necessary. I'll do all the work that must be done, but I shall not so much as hint at friendly relations, I'll be the boss, stingy and thrifty, I'll be a shark and a leech if need be. They'll respect me all the more. And this, surely, is the main thing – real respect.'

'Damn it all,' I said to myself. 'It all sounds as if they were getting ready to march against enemy tribes. A sort of war council, that is.'

'Well,' said a third man – a charming man, as a matter of fact – to me: 'Suppose I made myself a member of some peasant organization, and the village council ordered me to be flogged or something or other. What then?'

'And even if it did,' I wanted suddenly to say, but did not, because I was afraid to. (What is this? Why are we still sometimes afraid to express some of our thoughts?) 'Even if the council did give that order,' I thought to myself, 'and

---

[1]Kokoshnik – head-dress traditionally worn by Russian women. *Tr. note.*

15

they did flog you, what of it? Professors of aesthetics call such a turn of events the tragic side of life – and that is all there is to it. Surely a little thing like that does not warrant a whole life spent aloof from everyone else? Oh no, if we want to be all together let us really *all* be together, and if we want to be aloof let us be completely aloof. Elsewhere people had been through a good deal worse – women and children, too.

'Come, come now, women and children indeed!' my opponent would exclaim, 'the village council might have me flogged just like that, for no reason at all, because of another man's cow, perhaps, that had crashed into someone's else's vegetable garden, and you – you set it out as a general proposition.'

It sounds funny, of course, and, besides, it is a funny business altogether, a dirty business. I don't want to soil my hands with it. It's hardly decent even to talk of it. To hell with them all; let them all be whipped so far as I am concerned. It has nothing to do with me. As a matter of fact, so far as I am concerned, I can absolutely answer for the village council. My charming controversialist would not get so much as one little whack if it were possible to deal with him according to the council's decision. 'Let's take a money fine off him, fellows. He's gentry after all – not used to this sort of thing. Now, we are a different matter; our backsides are made for flogging.' That is how the council would decide, in the words of the village mayor in one of Stchedrin's provincial sketches. . .[1]

'Reaction!' someone will cry on reading this. 'Fancy putting up a defence of flogging!' (Honest to God, someone will deduce from this that I am standing up for

[1] N. Stchedrin, literary pseudonym of Michael Saltykov (1826–89), probably the most famous of all Russian satirists after Gogol. His *Provincial Sketches* were published in 1856/7 and gained for him an immediate and widespread popularity among the more liberal elements of the Russian reading public. *Tr. note.*

flogging.)

'Come now,' another man may say. 'What are you talking about? You wanted to tell us about Paris and now you have gone right off the track to tell us about flogging. What has Paris got to do with it?'

'What's all this?' a third man might add. 'You admit yourself that you heard about these things quite recently, yet you were travelling in the summer. How then could you have thought about all this in your railway carriage?'

'Quite right,' I would reply, 'this really is a problem. But let me see now, these are winter reminiscences of summer impressions. And some winter impressions got mixed up with the winter reminiscences. Besides as the train was approaching Eydtkuhnen my thoughts were particularly concentrated on all things Russian which I was abandoning for the sake of seeing Europe, and I remember meditating in that strain. The theme of my reflections was in fact the following: What kind of imprint did Europe leave on us at different times? Why did it constantly try to gatecrash upon us with its civilization? How civilized have we become and precisely how many of us have so far become civilized? I can now see that all this is somehow unnecessary. But then I did warn you beforehand that the whole chapter was unnecessary. But anyway, where did I stop? Oh, yes! Discussing a French coat! That is what it all started with.

Well now, one of these French coats at the time wrote *The Brigadier*.[1] *The Brigadier* was a marvellous thing by the standards then prevailing, and created an extraordinary effect. Potemkin himself said: 'You may as well die now, Denis, never will you write anything better.'[2] People began to stir as if roused from sleep. I wonder, I continued, letting my thoughts take their own course,

[1]See note I, page 8.
[2]Potemkin is supposed to have said this to Fonvizin at the first night of the play (1766). *Tr. note.*

were people even then tired of doing nothing, tired of a life in leading strings? I do not mean merely the French leading strings of the time, and would anyway like to add that we are a very credulous nation and that it all comes of our being so good-natured. We might, for instance, be all sitting idly round doing nothing and then suddenly take it into our heads that somebody had said or done something worthwhile. We might imagine that we, too, could be original and that we have found something to do, and then we would all get excited in the absolute conviction that now it is all going to begin. A fly might buzz past, and we are quite ready to take it for an elephant. It is of course due to youthful inexperience and dearth of native tradition. In Russia that sort of behaviour can be traced almost further back than *The Brigadier*, though it was then naturally only in its rudimentary stages, but it continues to the present day: we find something to do and then give squeals of delight. Squealing and bursting from sheer delight – that's what we really go in for. And yet, a couple of years later we slink off again, looking sheepish. But we never get tired and are always ready to begin again.

As to other leading strings, practically no one in Fonvizin's time had the slightest doubt that these were the most sacred, the most European of leading strings and the best of all possible tutelage. Of course, there are few doubters, even now. The whole of our ultra-progressive party is frantically in favour of foreign leading strings. But then, oh then it was a time of such faith in all kinds of leading strings that it is a wonder we did not move mountains then; it is odd indeed that all these Alaun downs and Pargolovo heights and Valdai peaks of ours still stand where they have always stood. True enough, a poet of the time did say about one of his characters that

Mountains groaned when he lay on them

18

and that

He cast towers high over clouds.

But that, it seems, was merely a metaphor.[1]

By the way, my dear sirs, I have only one type of literature in mind at the moment – the type known as *belles lettres*. It is through literature that I want to trace Europe's gradual and beneficial influence on our country. Just what books were then (before, and at the same time as, *The Brigadier*) published and read we cannot even conceive without feeling rather pleasantly superior! We now have a most remarkable writer, the pride of our time, a certain Kozma Prutkov.[2] His only defect consists in a modesty that passeth all understanding: he has not yet published his complete works. Well now, a long time ago he wrote *Sketches by my Grandfather*, which appeared in a miscellany published by *The Contemporary*. Just imagine the sort of thing that could have been written at the time by this debonair septuagenarian, who had lived in the reign of Catherine the Great, who had seen a thing or two in his life, who had been at court, who had fought at Ochakov and who had now retired to his ancestral farm and taken to writing his memoirs.[3] He certainly had something to write about, that man – all the things he had witnessed in his life!

---

[1] These two lines occur in Derzhavin's ode *On Suvorov's Victories* (1794) celebrating the taking of Warsaw by the Russian troops. Gabriel Derzhavin (1743–1816) – statesman and Grand Old Man of Russian eighteenth-century poetry. *Tr. note.*

[2] Kozma Prutkov – imaginary civil servant and author of bogus aphorisms, comic verse, fables, anecdotes, etc. The pseudonym was used by the poet Alexey Tolstoy (1817–71) and his cousins Zhemchuzhnikov. *Tr. note.*

[3] Ochakov – a fortress (now town) on the north shore of the Black Sea, captured by Potemkin from the Turks in 1788. *Tr. note.*

Yet his book is composed entirely of such little stories as the following:

THE WITTY ANSWER OF THE CHEVALIER DE MONTBAZON

A very attractive young lady once coolly asked the Chevalier de Montbazon in the King's presence: 'Can you tell me, my lord, whether a dog is attached to its tail or the tail to the dog?' To which the Chevalier, being quick at repartee and therefore not in the slightest confused, replied in an even tone of voice: 'There is no rule, Madam, forbidding a man to catch a dog either by its tail or by its head.' This reply gave the King much pleasure and the Chevalier did not go unrewarded.

You think that all this is stuff and nonsense, and that an old man like that never really existed in this world. But I promise you that when I was ten years old, I myself and with my own eyes read a book written in the Great Catherine's time which contained the following story:

THE WITTY ANSWER OF THE CHEVALIER DE ROHAN

It is a well known fact that the Chevalier de Rohan suffered from very bad breath. One day when he was present at a levee of the Prince de Condé, the latter said to him: 'Do not stand quite so near, Chevalier, for you smell most unpleasantly.' To which the Chevalier immediately gave answer: 'Not I, your most gracious Highness, but rather you, for you have just come out of bed.'

Now, just try and imagine that old man living on his land, a seasoned warrior who had lost an arm perhaps, surrounded by his old wife, his country-bumpkin children and a hundred servants, steaming himself every Saturday in his Russian bath till he is purple in the face. There he is with his glasses on his nose, gravely and enthusiastically reading this kind of story and imagining it to be the very essence of culture into the bargain; indeed, thinking himself almost in duty bound to read it. What a naïve faith they then had in the utility of such news from Europe and the necessity of it. 'It is,' they said, 'a well-known fact that the Chevalier de Rohan suffered from bad breath.' To whom was it well known? Why was it well known? What bumpkins somewhere in the backwoods of Russia knew it so well? And anyway who would want to know it? But such revolutionary thoughts never disturbed the old man. With the most childlike faith he would decide that this 'collection of witty stories' was well known at court, and that would be quite sufficient so far as he was concerned.

Oh, certainly we found it easy to assimilate Europe then – in the physical sense, of course. It was difficult to avoid using the whip when it came to moral assimilation. People would put on silk stockings and wigs, attach swords to themselves – and look for all the world like Europeans. And not only was it not felt as an encumbrance, but it was, in fact, liked. And yet in practice everything remained as before: once Rohan (of whom all that was known was that he had very bad breath) was laid aside and spectacles were taken off, people still dealt with their servants – as before, their attitude to their family was still as patriarchal – as before, they still had the neighbouring farmer thrashed in the stables – as before – if he was poorer than they and happened to say something rude, still demeaned them-selves in the presence of their superiors – as before. Even the peasant understood it all better: his masters despised him less, held his customs and habits in less contempt, knew more about him, were not strangers to him to the same extent, not foreigners quite as much. And as to them throwing their weight about in his presence, what else could you expect? That's what they were the masters for. They may have thrashed their peasants to death, but the people liked them better all the same, because they were nearer to them somehow. In fact all these fellows were simple, sturdy folk, never in anything tried to go to the root of the matter, grabbed, thrashed, stole, fondly sweated their peasants, and went through life peacefully in fat contentment and 'in conscientious and childish debauch'.[1] I even suspect that all those grandfathers of ours were not all that innocent, even in that little matter of the Rohans and the Montbazons.

Some of them were great rogues even, and knew their own worth when it came to all these European influences from above. All that fantastic make-believe, all that masquerading, all those French coats, cuffs, wigs, swords, all those fat, clumsy legs, thrust into silk stockings, those little soldiers in German wigs and boots, all this, it seems to me, was a great swindle, so that even the simple people sometimes noticed it and understood. Of course one can be a clerk or a swindler or a brigadier and yet be innocently and touchingly convinced that the Chevalier de Rohan is in fact the very embodiment of the most exquisite refinement. But then this did not prevent anyone from behaving as they always did: the Gvozdilovs bullied as they had always done.[2] Our Potemkin and others of his ilk very nearly had our Rohans thrashed in their stables, our Montbazons fleeced the quick and the dead, boxed people's ears with lace-cuffed fists and kicked their backsides with silk-stockinged feet, and our marquises at court levees rolled about on the floor,

[1]Quotation from the poem *Meditation* by Lermontov (1814–41). *Tr. note.*

[2]Gvozdilov – one of the characters in Fonvizin's play *The Brigadier* (see note 1, page 8). According to the conventions of the time, his personality is revealed by his name, which is derived from the word *gvozdit*, to beat or bully. *Tr. note.*

In valiant disregard of bumps on their heads.[1]

In short all this Europe, bespoke and to order, managed surprisingly well to achieve a harmonious co-existence among us, beginning with St Petersburg – the most fantastic town with the most fantastic history of all towns on this planet.

But nowadays it is no longer the same, and St Petersburg has triumphed. Nowadays we have come up to standard and are fully fledged Europeans. Nowadays Gvozdilov himself uses skill when doing his bullying, keeps up appearances, is becoming a French bourgeois and before long will take to quoting texts to defend the slave trade like any American from the Southern States of the USA.

As a matter of fact, the habit of quoting texts in self-defence is now increasingly reaching Europe from the United States. When I get there, I said to myself, I shall see it with my own eyes. You can never learn from books as much as you can see with your own eyes.

By the way, talking of Gvozdilov: Why did Fonvizin put one of the most remarkable phrases in his *Brigadier* not into the mouth of Sophia, who in that comedy represents the idea of noble, humane and European progress, but into the mouth of the brigadier's inane wife, whom he made into such a fool (and a reactionary fool at that, not just a fool) that all the threads are there for everyone to see and all the inanities she says seem to be said not by her, but by someone else hiding behind her back? But when the truth had to be said, it was not Sophia who said it, but the brigadier's wife. After all, he made her not only into a perfect fool, but into a bad woman as well; and yet he seemed afraid, and even considered it artistically impossible, that such a phrase should pop out of the mouth of

---

[1]Quotation from Griboyedov's comedy of manners *Woe from Wit* (1824). *Tr. note.*

Sophia, with her hot-house plant upbringing. Instead, he apparently considered it more natural that it should have been uttered by a simple, stupid woman. Here is the passage, it is worth recalling. It is very curious and is made so by the fact that it was written with no end in view, not even tongue in cheek, naïvely and perhaps even accidentally. The brigadier's wife says to Sophia:

. . . We had a captain in our regiment who commanded No. 1 Company. His name was Gvozdilov and he had such a pretty little wife. Well now, would you believe it, my dear, whenever he lost his temper or was drunk rather, he used to bully her within an inch of her life and would never tell her what for. It was none of my business, of course, but I used to weep my eyes out sometimes, looking at her.

SOPHIA: Pray, Madam, stop telling us things so revolting to humanity.

BRIGADIER'S WIFE: There you are, my dear, you don't even want to *hear* about it, and how do you think the captain's wife felt, who had to *bear* it?

Thus, for all her good manners and sensibility Sophia is made to look a fool by the side of a simple and common woman. This is one of Fonvizin's remarkable repartees (or retorts), and he has nothing neater, more human, and . . . more accidental. And we still have a countless number of such hot-house progressives among the most advanced of our public men, who are very well satisfied with their hot-houses and demand nothing better. But the most remarkable thing of all is that Gvozdilov still bullies his wife and does it almost in greater comfort than before. He does, really. They say it used to be done in greater amity and with more kindness! To love is to thrash, says the proverb. Wives, they say, became quite worried if they

24

were not beaten: 'he doesn't beat me, means he doesn't love me,' they said.

But all this is primitive and elemental, harking back to the times of our ancestors. Nowadays even this is subject to progress. Nowadays Gvozdilov bullies almost out of principle, and then only because he is still a fool, that is an old-fashioned man who has failed to keep up with the times. The reason why I expatiate on the theme of Gvozdilov is that people in this country still write paragraphs about him full of profound meaning and human understanding. And they write so much that the public is tired of them. Gvozdilov is sufficiently tenacious of life to be almost immortal. Oh, yes, he is alive and kicking, drunk and replete. Now he has only one arm and one leg left and, like Captain Kopeykin, 'had shed his blood, in a manner of speaking'.[1] His wife has long ago ceased to be the 'pretty young thing' she used to be. She has grown old, and her face is pale, haggard and furrowed by wrinkles and suffering. But when her husband, the captain, lay ill after the loss of his arm, she never left his bedside, spent sleepless nights watching over him, comforted him, wept bitter tears over him, and called him her dear, her valiant knight, the darling of her heart, her own soldier bold and brave. It may, oh it may, arouse our indignation from one point of view. But from another – long live the Russian woman! There is nothing better in our Russian world than her limitlessly forgiving love. For that is so, is it not? Particularly as nowadays Gvozdilov, too, when he is sober, does not always beat his wife, or rather beats her less frequently, keeps up a semblance of decency and even has an occasional tender word for her. For he has become aware in his old age that he cannot do without her; he is thrifty and bourgeois, and if he does give her a beating even now, it is only when he is drunk or

[1]Kopeykin – a character in Gogol's *Dead Souls* (1842). *Tr. note.*

25

else out of habit, when he feels bored. And this certainly is progress, whatever you say; which is a comfort. And we love so much being comforted.

Oh yes, we are quite comforted now and we have succeeded in comforting ourselves. It may be that reality around us looks none too lovely even yet; but then we are so wonderful ourselves, so civilized, so European that the common people feel sick at the very sight of us. We have now reached the point when the common people regard us as complete foreigners, and do not understand a single word of ours, a single look of ours, a single thought of ours – and this certainly is progress, whatever you say. We have now reached the point where our contempt for the common people and the basic principles of its being, is so profound that even our attitude to it is stamped with a new, unprecedented and kind of supercilious disdain which did not exist even at the time of our Montbazons and Rohans, and this certainly is progress, whatever you say.

And then how self-confident we now are in our civilizing mission, with what an air of superiority we solve all problems, and what problems! There is no soil, we say, and no people, nationality is nothing but a certain system of taxation, the soul is a *tabula rasa*, a small piece of wax out of which you can readily mould a real man, a world man or a humunculus – all that must be done is to apply the fruits of European civilization and read two or three books.[1] And then how serene, how majestically serene we are, because we have solved all problems and written them off.

[1]This passage is one of Dostoyevsky's earliest allusions to the version of Slavophilism to which his periodical *Vremya* was dedicated. Known as *pochvennichestvo* (from *pochva*, soil), it aimed at reconciling Slavophil and Westernizing tendencies in Russian thought. Overladen though it is by foreign Western influences, Russia, argued Dostoyevsky, must nevertheless strive to evolve its own indigenous cultural expression of 'idea', derived from its native soil. Far from repudiating the West, this 'Russian idea', according to Dostoyevsky, 'will perhaps be the synthesis of all the ideas developed in [Western] Europe'. *Tr. note.*

With what smug self-satisfaction, for instance, we have trounced Turgenev for his refusal to make his peace with the world together with us, for his refusal to be satisfied with our majestic personalities and accept them as his ideal, and for having sought something better than us. Better than us, good God! But what can be lovelier and more faultless than us in this sublunar world? He certainly got into hot water over Bazarov, Bazarov restless and troubled (sign of a great heart) despite all his nihilism. We have even trounced him for his Kukshina, for that progressive louse which Turgenev had combed out of Russian reality for us to look at, and we accused him of opposing the emancipation of women into the bargain.[1] All this is certainly progress, whatever you say.

Now we stand over the common people with the self-assurance of corporals or sergeant-majors of civilization. It is a delight to look at us: arms akimbo and glance defiant, we look really cocky, and we say to the peasant with all the contempt we can muster: 'Nationality and national community all boil down to political reaction and the assessment of taxes, so what have you to teach us, you old lout?' For really we cannot be expected to pander to prejudice.

Oh Goodness me . . . Let us assume for a minute, my dear sirs, that my travels are over and I am back in Russia, and let me tell you a story. One day this autumn, as I was reading a newspaper – one of the most progressive ones – I noticed the following news from Moscow. Heading: 'More relics of barbarism' (or something like this, very

---

[1]Bazarov – a character in Turgenev's *Fathers and Sons* (1861) representing extreme materialism and opposition to accepted prejudices and opinions. He is the Russian literary symbol of nihilism, a term popularized by Turgenev though not, as is sometimes said, coined by him.

Kukshina, another character in the same novel, is meant to represent the prototype of the mid-nineteenth-century 'emancipated woman', with ideas similar to those of Bazarov. *Tr. note..*

sharply worded. Unfortunately, however, I haven't got the newspaper in front of me now). Well anyway, the story as told there was that one morning this autumn an open carriage was espied in the streets of Moscow. A drunken woman – a professional match-maker by occupation – was sitting in the carriage all beribboned and singing a song. The coachman was also bedecked in some sort of ribbons, was also drunk and was also caterwauling as best he could. Even the horse was adorned with ribbons. I don't know, though, whether it was drunk. It probably was. The woman was holding a bundle, the contents of which she was going to exhibit and which belonged to a newly married couple who had obviously passed a happy night together. The bundle, of course, contained a certain light garment which, among the lower classes, is usually shown the following day to the bride's parents. People laughed at the sight of the match-maker woman and a gay sight it was. Indignantly, forcefully and contemptuously the newspaper related this unheard of barbarism 'which has survived to this day in spite of the progress of civilization!'

I admit that I burst out laughing. Oh please, do not think that I am trying to defend primitive cannibalism, light garments, veils, etc. It is bad, it is unchaste, it is uncivilized, it is Slav. I know all that and I agree; though of course it was not done with evil intent, but merely as part of marriage celebrations and out of natural simplicity and ignorance of anything better, loftier, more European. Oh no, I laughed at something else. I laughed because I suddenly remembered our ladies and our fashionable dress shops. Of course civilized ladies no longer send their light garments to their parents, but when it comes to ordering a dress at a dressmaker's, how cunningly and efficiently they know how to pad certain parts of their charming European dress with cotton-wool. What is the cotton-wool for? Naturally for the sake of elegance and aesthetic effect, *pour paraître* . . . Not only that: their daughters too, these innocent, seventeen-year-old young things just out of school, even they know about the cotton-wool. They know everything: the purpose of that cotton-wool and where precisely, in which parts to apply the cotton-wool, and they know, too, why – that is, with what end in view – all this is being used . . . Well now, I chuckled inwardly, all the care and trouble that is being taken, *conscious* care about these cotton-wool additions, is it really purer, more moral and more chaste than the wretched light garment taken with such naïve certainty to the parent, the certainty that that is precisely what is called for, precisely the moral thing to do?

For Heaven's sake, my friends, do not think I now want to read you a lecture to the effect that civilization is not progress and that latterly in Europe it has on the contrary always threatened all progress with whip and prison. Do not think that I shall try to prove that in our country we barbarously confuse civilization with the laws of normal and true progress, or that civilization has long ago been condemned even in the West, and that its one and only advocate over there is the capitalist (though everyone there is a capitalist or wants to be one) because he wants to save his money.

Do not think that I shall try to prove that the human soul is not a *tabula rasa*, a piece of wax to be moulded into a pan-homunculus; that the primary need is for nature, then for science, then for independent unrestricted life deeply rooted in the soil, and finally for faith in one's own national powers.

Do not think I shall pretend to be ignorant of the fact that our progressively minded men (though by no means all of them) are no defenders of cotton-wool and, in fact, brand it as they brand light garments.

All I want to say now is that the article had an ulterior motive for censuring and condemning the light garments;

it did not state simply that it was barbarism, but was exposing elemental, national, working-class barbarism, in opposition to the European civilization of our aristocratic upper classes. The article swaggered, the article pretended not to know that those who were thus exposing this barbarism were themselves guilty of things perhaps a thousand times worse and filthier or that all we had done was to exchange one kind of prejudice and nastiness for another, worse kind of prejudice and nastiness. The article pretended not to notice our own prejudice and nastiness. Why then, why should we look so cocky as we stand over the common people, arms akimbo, breathing contempt. . . For this faith in infallibility and in the right to make these exposures is absurd, laughably absurd. This faith is either simply swagger to impress the people or else an unreasoning, slavish worship of the European forms of civilization; and this, surely, is even more absurd.

But what's the use! Thousands of such facts could be found every day. Forgive me my little story.

However, *mea culpa*. For I *have* committed a fault. The reason is that I have jumped too hastily from grandfathers to grandsons. There were other facts in between. Remember Chatsky.[1] He was neither an artlessly wily grandfather nor a self-satisfied grandson; cocky and sure of himself, Chatsky was quite a special type of our Russian Europe, a pleasant, enthusiastic, suffering type, appealing to Russia

[1]Chatsky – the main character of Griboyedov's play *Woe from Wit*, probably modelled on Chaadayev (see note 1, page 9). He represents honesty and common-sense with disastrous consequences to himself. Treated as insane by his former friends at a ball given by Famusov, he shakes off the dust of Moscow and makes his exit with a speech in which occurs the phrase about 'wounded pride' quoted below. Famusov, Skalozub, Repetilov, Molchalin, Countess Khlestov, Natalia Dmitriyevna (a slip on Dostoyevsky's part – it should be Natalia Yuriyevna) – names mentioned in this chapter – are all characters out of the same play. *Tr. note.*

and to firm foundations, and yet going back to Europe again when he had to find

A place of refuge for man's wounded pride . . .

in fact a type which is useless now, but which was terribly useful in the past. He was a phrase-monger, a chatterbox, but a kind phrase-monger, sincerely sorry for his uselessness. Now in the new generation he is reborn and, we believe, in youthful vigour. We trust that he will appear once again, but this time not suffering from hysteria as at Famusov's ball, but as a conqueror, proud, mighty, meek and loving. Besides, he will have realized by then that the place of refuge for wounded pride is to be found not in Europe, but perhaps under his very nose, and he will find something to do and will do it.

And do you know what? I, for one, am convinced we haven't only got sergeants of civilization and European fadists; I am convinced, I insist, that the new man is born already . . . but more of this later. Now I want to say a bit more about Chatsky. There is one thing I cannot understand. Chatsky was surely a very intelligent man. How is it that such an intelligent man failed to find himself a job of work to do? As a matter of fact, none of them had ever found themselves jobs of work to do, they failed to find them for twenty-three generations running. This is a fact, and it is surely no use arguing against facts, but one may always ask a question out of curiosity. Well now, I cannot understand how an intelligent man can fail, at any time and in any circumstances, to find himself a job of work to do. This, I am told, is arguable, but in my heart of hearts I do not believe it is. We are given intelligence in order to achieve our aims. If you cannot walk a mile, then walk at least a hundred steps; it would anyway be better than nothing, or at least nearer your object if you have an object to go to. But if you insist on reaching your object step by step this is not, in my estimation, intelligence. You could even be called work-shy in that case. We do not like toil, are not used to take one step at a time and prefer to reach our object or become a second Regulus in one flying leap. But this is precisely to be work-shy.

However, Chatsky was perfectly right at the time to slip away abroad again; a little delay would have sent him Eastwards instead of Westwards. People love the West in this country; they love it and when it comes to a certain point they all go there. I am going there too, as you see. *Mais moi, c'est autre chose.* I saw them all there, many of them that is; there is no keeping count of them all, and all of them seem to be seeking a refuge for wounded pride. In any case they are seeking something.

The generation of Chatskys of both sexes after Famusov's ball, and generally speaking when the ball was over, increased and multiplied till they were as numerous out there as the sands of the sea. And not even the Chatskys alone: for everyone left Moscow to go abroad. There are Goodness knows how many Repetilovs and Skalozubs there, retired by now and despatched to a watering place as unfit for further work. Natalia Dmitriyevna and her husband are life members of these institutions. Even Countess Khlestov is taken there every year. All these people are tired even of Moscow. Molchalin alone is not among them; he has made other arrangements and remained at home, the only one to have done so. He has, so to say, dedicated himself to his country, to his fatherland. . . .He is unattainable now and wouldn't let Famusov inside his door: 'Country neighbours, the Famusovs, not the people to greet in town'. He is in business and has found himself a job of work to do. He lives in St Petersburg and . . . and has been successful. 'He knows Russia and Russia knows him.' Oh yes, knows him well and will not forget him in a hurry. He is not even silent now; on the contrary, he is the only one to speak. He is the expert . . .

But enough of him! I mentioned them all, saying that they were trying to find a happy spot in Europe, and really I thought they preferred it there. But in fact their faces register such bored melancholy . . . Poor things! How restless they all are, how morbidly and sadly always on the move! They all walk about with guide-books and rush greedily in every town to see the sights, do it, indeed, as if in duty bound or as if they were still performing their State service: they would never miss a single palace – be it only three-window size – if only it is mentioned in the guide-book, not a single town-mayor's residence, very similar to the most ordinary Moscow or Petersburg house; they stare at Rubens' meaty carcasses and believe that they represent the three graces because their guide-books bid them believe it; they rush at the Sistine Madonna and stand in front of her in bovine expectation, the expectation that something will happen any minute now, that somebody will crawl out from underneath the floor and dispel their aimless, bored melancholy and fatigue. And then they go off surprised because nothing has happened. This is not the self-satisfied and perfectly mechanical curiosity of British tourists – men and women – who look more into their guide-books than at the sights, do not expect anything either new or extraordinary and merely check to see what the guide-book has to say and precisely how many feet or pounds any particular object measures or weighs. Our own curiosity is somehow savage, nervous, frantically eager, yet secretly convinced in advance that nothing will ever happen – of course, till the very next fly that happens to buzz past when it all begins again.

And I am now talking of intelligent people only. It is no use worrying about the others – God always looks after them – or about those who have made their home there, who are gradually forgetting their mother-tongue and begin to listen to catholic priests.[1] However, there is only one thing to be said about the whole lot of them: as soon as we get beyond Eydtkuhnen we all of us immediately become startingly similar to those wretched little dogs which run about when they loose their master.

You don't imagine, do you, that I am sneering at anyone, or blaming somebody because 'at the present time when etc. you remain abroad! The peasant problem is in full swing, and you remain abroad!' and so on and so forth? Oh not at all, not in the slightest. Besides, who am I to blame anyone? Whom should I blame and for what? 'We would like to do some useful work, but there is no work, and what there is of it is being done without us anyway. All the jobs have been taken and there are no vacancies in view. It's no use trying to barge in where there is no call for you.' That's their whole excuse and not a very impressive one at that. Besides, we know that excuse by heart.

But what is this? Where did I get to? How have I had time to see the Russians abroad? We are only coming into Eydtkuhnen . . . Or have passed it by now. In fact we have; Berlin and Dresden and Cologne – we have passed them all. It is true I am still sitting in a railway carriage, but before us is Erquelines, and not Eydtkuhnen and we are entering France. Paris, it's Paris I wanted to talk about – and forgot. That's because I let my thoughts wander on the subject of our Russian Europe; which is forgivable in a man who is himself on the way to visiting European Europe. But anyway, there is not need to insist on being forgiven. This chapter of mine is superfluous, as you will remember.

[1] No doubt an oblique reference to Prince Ivan Gagarin who left Russia in 1843 and made his home in France, where he was converted to Catholicism and joined the Jesuit Order. His conversion made a great impression on Dostoyevsky, who refers to it in later works. *Tr. note.*

CHAPTER IV

WHICH IS NOT SUPERFLUOUS FOR
TRAVELLERS
FINAL VERDICT ON THE IRRATIONALITY
OF FRENCHMEN

'BUT WHY IS IT, after all, that Frenchmen are not rational?'

I asked myself this question as I was examining four new passengers, Frenchmen, who had just come into our carriage. They were the first Frenchmen I met on their native soil if I discount the customs officials in Erquelines which we had just left. The customs officials had been exceedingly polite, did their job quickly and I entered my carriage very pleased with my début in France.

As far as Erquelines, though our compartment had eight seats, there were only two of us: myself and a Swiss, a middle-aged man, simple and reserved, and a pleasant conversationalist at that, so that we chatted all the time for about two hours on end. But now there were six of us, and to my astonishment my Swiss at the sight of our four new companions fell, all of a sudden, almost completely silent. I made an attempt to continue our conversation, but he was obviously eager to change the subject, gave short non-commital answers, turned away from me with an air almost of annoyance, gazed at the view out of the window for a bit and then, taking out his German guide-book, was soon entirely absorbed in it. I abandoned him at once and without saying a word concentrated my attention on our new companions.

They were odd folk, somehow. They carried no luggage and bore not the slightest resemblance to travellers. They did not have so much as a bundle between them nor were they dressed in a way calculated to make them look like travellers. They all wore a thin sort of frock-coat, terribly shabby and threadbare, little better than those worn by our officers' batmen or by servants in the house of a not very well-off country squire. Their shirts were dirty, their neck-ties very bright and also very dirty; one of them wore the remnants of a silk kerchief, of the kind which are constantly worn and become stiff with grease after fifteen years' contact with the wearer's neck. The man also had studs with imitation diamonds the size of a hazel nut. However, there was a certain smartness and even dash about them. All four appeared to be of the same age – thirty-five or thereabout – and though their faces were dissimilar, they themselves were very much alike. Their faces, somewhat haggard in appearance, had the usual little French beards which also looked very much alike. They were obviously people with a large and varied experience behind them, who had acquired a permanently business-like, if sour, expression. Also, I got the impression that they knew each other but I do not remember them exchanging a single word. It was fairly obvious that they did not want to look at us – that is, at the Swiss and at me – they sat and smoked with a somewhat nonchalant air and affected complete indifference, as they riveted their gaze on the windows of the compartment.

I lit a cigarette and began to examine them for lack of anything better to do. True enough, the question did flit through my mind – what sort of people can they possibly be? Not quite workmen, but not quite bourgeois either. Could they possibly be ex-soldiers? Something *à demi-solde* perhaps? However, I did not worry about them too much. Ten minutes later, as soon as we reached the next station, all four of them jumped out of the train one after another, the door slammed and we sped on. Along this route the train hardly waits at the stations: about two minutes, three at the most, and on it rushes. The transport is excellent, in other words – very quick.

As soon as we remained alone the Swiss immediately shut his guide-book, put it aside and looked at me with an air of satisfaction, obviously keen to renew our conversation.

'Those fellows did not stay long,' I began, looking at him with some curiosity.

'But they only intended to travel till the next station.'

'Do you know them?'

'Them? . . . Why, they are the police . . .'

'How do you mean? What police?' I asked with surprise.

'There now . . . I noticed at once you had no idea who they were.'

'And . . . are they really police spies?' (I still could not bring myself to believe it.)

'Of course; they came in here because of us.'

'You know it for certain?'

'Oh, there's no doubt about it. I have travelled this way several times before. We were pointed out to them back in the customs house while our passports were being examined, our names were told to them and so on and so forth. So they came and sat down here in order to accompany us.'

'But why should they, after all, want to accompany us if they have seen us already? You said, didn't you, that we were pointed out to them at that other station?'

'We were indeed, and our names given. but that's not enough. Now they have studied us in detail: face, dress, suitcases, in fact our whole appearance. They have made a mental note of your studs; you took out your cigar-case, if you remember – well now, they've made a note of that cigar-case, too; all these little trifles, you know, and distinguishing marks, particularly distinguishing marks – as many of them as possible. You could lose yourself in Paris, or change your name (if you are a suspicious character, that is). Those trifles would then help the search. All this is immediately telegraphed to Paris from the very same station. And there it's kept in the proper place, in case of need. Besides, hotel keepers must supply the most detailed information about foreigners, and must include trifles as well!'

'But why,' I went on asking, still feeling a bit puzzled, 'were there so many of them? There were four of them, after all!'

'Oh, they are very numerous here. Probably this time there are few foreigners, but if there were more they would have distributed themselves among different coaches.'

'Come now, they did not even look at us. They were looking out of the windows.'

'Oh, don't you worry, they saw everything . . . It was because of us they sat down here.'

Well, well, I thought, there you are, you and your 'irrational Frenchmen', and I threw (shamefacedly, I admit) a somewhat mistrustful glance at the Swiss, as the thought flitted through my mind: you wouldn't be one of those yourself, my boy, would you now, and just pretending not to be? But I did not think that for more than a split second, I assure you. Absurd, but what can one do? Such thoughts are bound to arise. . . .

The Swiss had told me the truth. As soon as I arrived at my hotel a full description of my person down to the most intimate detail was immediately made and sent to the appropriate authorities. The thoroughness and minuteness with which you are examined in order to describe all particulars concerning you lead one to conclude that your entire life in the hotel, your every step, so to speak, is being scrupulously observed and counted. However, in my first hotel I, personally, was not bothered and my description was drawn up on the quiet, except, of course, for the questions which you are asked in the book in which you make your full confession: Who are you, how did you arrive and whence and with what intentions in mind? etc. But in the second hotel to which I went, having failed to find a room in my first – the Hôtel des Coquillières – after my eight-day trip to London, I was treated with far greater frankness. In general this second hotel – Hôtel des Empereurs – seemed to be run much more on family lines in every respect. The owner and his wife were very good people and very considerate, rather elderly and extraordinarily attentive to the needs of their guests. In the evening of the very day on which I arrived the landlady caught me in the hall and asked me to come into the room which served as an office. The husband was there too, but the landlady apparently ran the whole administrative side.

'I am sorry,' she began politely, 'we need all your particulars.'

'But I've given them to you . . . you have my passport.'

'Yes, but *votre état?*'

This '*votre état?*' is an extremely confusing thing and I never liked it. What can one put down? Traveller is too abstract. *Homme de lettres* earns no respect.

'We'd better put down *propriétaire*. What do you think?' asked the landlady. 'That would be best of all.'

'Oh yes, that would be best of all,' confirmed her spouse.

'All right. Well now, your reason for visiting Paris?'

'As a traveller, in transit.'

'Mm . . . yes, *pour voir Paris*. Now, monsieur, your height?'

'How do you mean – height?'

'How tall are you, in fact?'

'Average height – as you can see.'

'That's so, monsieur . . . But we should like to know a bit more precisely. . . . I should think, I should think . . .' she went on, looking questioningly at her husband.

'I should think *so high*,' decided the husband, stating my height in metres as a rough estimate.

'But what do you want it for?' I asked.

'Oh, it is es-sential,' replied the landlady with a polite drawl on the word 'essential', but at the same time entering my height in the book. 'Now, monsieur, your hair? Fair . . . e-er . . . very fair, really . . . straight . . .'

She made a note of the hair as well.

'Would you mind, monsieur,' she went on as she put down her pen, left her seat and came up to me with all the politeness she could muster, 'over here, a step or two nearer the window. I must have a look at the colour of your eyes. Hm . . . light colour . . .'

And again she glanced questioningly at her husband. They were obviously very fond of each other.

'A bit greyish,' remarked the husband with a particuarly business-like, even worried expression. 'Voilà,' he said and gave his wife a wink, pointing at something over one of his eyebrows, but I understood perfectly well what it was he was pointing at. I have a small scar on my forehead and he wanted his wife to take note of this distinguishing mark, too.

'Permit me to ask you now,' I said to the landlady when the whole examination was over, 'are you really required to present such a detailed account?'

'Oh, monsieur, it is es-sential! . . .'

'Monsieur!' repeated the husband after her, with a somehow particularly impressive air.

'But they didn't ask me in the Hôtel de Coquillières.'

'Impossible,' retorted the landlady promptly. 'They could get into serious trouble for that. They probably examined you without saying a word about it, but they certainly, certainly examined you. But we are simpler and more frank with our guests. We treat them as members of the family. You will be satisfied with us. You'll see . . .'

'Oh, monsieur! . . .' confirmed the husband solemnly and a look of tenderness even came over his face.

And this was a very honest and a very pleasant couple,

anyway as far as I got to know them afterwards. But the word 'es-sential' was pronounced by no means apologetically or in a tone of voice which pleaded extenuating circumstances, but rather in the sense of absolute necessity which almost coincided with their personal convictions.

And so I am in Paris.

Chapter V

BAAL

AND SO I AM IN PARIS. . . . Don't think, however, that I shall tell you a lot about Paris itself. I should think you have already read so much about it in Russian that you are tired of reading about it by now. Besides you have been there yourselves and have probably seen it all better than I have. I never could abide, when I was abroad, looking at things in the proper way as approved by the guide-books, as every good traveller should.

I am now ashamed to own up to the things I have sometimes missed in consequence. In Paris, too, I have missed seeing certain things. I shall not say what they were, but I will say one thing: I have found a definition for Paris, have selected an epithet for it and shall stand by this epithet. It is this: it is the most moral and the most virtuous town in the whole world. What order! What sweet reasonableness! What definite and firmly established relationships! How buttoned up and secure everything is! How perfectly pleased and happy they all are! And how hard they have all tried! – so hard that they have really convinced themselves that they are pleased and perfectly happy, and, and . . . have stopped there. There can be no further advance. You will never believe that they have stopped there; you will say that I exaggerate, that this is all a libel invented by a bilious patriot, that things could not in fact have stopped dead. But, my friends, I have warned you as far back as the first chapter of these notes, you

42

know, that I may tell dreadful lies. So don't stand in the way. You surely know too, that if I tell lies I shall tell them in the conviction that I am not telling them. Personally I think this should amply suffice you, and you had better give me full freedom.

Oh indeed, Paris is a remarkable town. And how much comfort and convenience is put at the disposal of those who have a right to comfort and convenience! And again, what order, what *stillness of order*, so to speak! I keep harking back to *order*. Indeed, a little longer and Paris with its one and a half million inhabitants will become like some small German university town, fossilized in stillness and order, something like Heidelberg, for example. It seems to be tending that way. And why shouldn't there be a Heidelberg on a colossal scale? And what regimentation! Don't misunderstand me: I don't mean, so much, external regimentation, which is insignificant (relatively, of course) but a colossal internal, spiritual regimentation having its sources in the very depths of the soul. Paris tries to contract, willingly, lovingly somehow tries to make itself smaller than it really is, tries to shrink within itself, smiling benignly as it does so.

Now London is in this respect something entirely different. I only spent eight days altogether in London and the impression it left upon my mind – superficially at least – was of something on a grand scale, of vivid planning, original and not forced into a common mould. Everything there is so vast and so harsh in its originality. This originality is even a bit deceptive. Every harshness and every inconsistency is able to live in harmony with its antithesis and persist in walking hand-in-hand with it, continuing to be inconsistent, but apparently by no means excluding its antithesis. Each part stoutly upholds its own way and apparently does not interfere with the other parts of the whole. And yet there too the same stubborn, silent and by now chronic struggle is carried on, the struggle to the death of the typically Western principle of individual isolation with the necessity to live in some sort of harmony with each other, to create some sort of community and to settle down in the same ant-hill; even turning into an ant-hill seems desirable – anything to be able to settle down without having to devour each other – the alternative is to turn into cannibals.

In this connection, however, both Paris and London have one thing in common: the same desperate yearning, born of despair, to retain the status quo, to tear out by the roots all desires and hopes they might harbour within them, to damn the future in which perhaps even the very leaders of progress lack faith, and to bow down in worship of Baal.

But please do not get carried away by this lofty language: all this can be consciously felt only in the minds of the more advanced and clear-headed individuals, and unconsciously and by instinct in the living, everyday actions of the masses. But the ordinary man, the bourgeois in Paris, for instance, is almost consciously well satisfied and convinced that everything is as it should be and may even beat you up if you express a doubt on that score. But he will do so because he is still a little nervous in spite of all his self-confidence.

In that way London is much the same, but what an overwhelming spectacle it presents, painted on a vast canvas. Even superficially, how different it is from Paris! The immense town, forever bustling by night and by day, as vast as an ocean, the screech and howl of machinery, the railways built above the houses (and soon to be built under them) the daring of enterprise, the apparent disorder which in actual fact is the highest form of bourgeois order, the polluted Thames, the coal-saturated air, the magnificent squares and parks, the town's terrifying districts such as Whitechapel with its half-naked, savage and hungry population, the City with its millions and its world-wide

44

trade, the Crystal Palace, the World Exhibition . . .[1]

The Exhibition is indeed amazing. You feel the terrible force which has brought these innumerable people, who have come from the ends of the earth, all together into one fold; you realize the grandeur of the idea; you feel that something has been achieved here, that here is victory and triumph. And you feel nervous. However great your independence of mind, a feeling of fear somehow creeps over you. Can this, you think, in fact be the final accomplishment of an ideal state of things? Is this the end, by any chance? Perhaps this really is the 'one fold'?[2] Perhaps we shall really have to accept this as the whole truth and cease from all movement thereafter? It is all so solemn, triumphant and proud that you are left breathless. You look at those hundreds of thousands, at those millions of people obediently trooping into this place from all parts of the earth – people who have come with only one thought in mind, quietly, stubbornly and silently milling round in this colossal palace, and you feel that something final has been accomplished here – accomplished and completed. It is a Biblical sight, something to do with Babylon, some prophecy out of the Apocalypse being fulfilled before your very eyes. You feel that a rich and ancient tradition of denial and protest is needed in order not to yield, not to succumb to impression, not to bow down in worship of fact, and not to idolize Baal, that is, not to take the actual for the ideal. . .

But this, you will say, is nonsense, morbid nonsense, nerves, exaggeration. No one will halt there and no one will take this for his ideal. Besides, hunger and slavery are no friends to anyone and will – no one better – suggest denial and give rise to scepticism. But dilettantes, replete and satisfied and strolling about for their own delectation

[1]See note 1, page 13.
[2]St John x, 16.

can, of course, conjure up pictures out of the Apocalypse and excite their nervous systems by exaggeration and by extorting powerful sensations out of every fact for the sake of auto-stimulation. . . .

All right, I reply, let us admit I had been carried away by the décor; I may have been. But if you had seen how proud the mighty spirit is which created that colossal décor and how convinced it is of its victory and its triumph, you would have shuddered at its pride, its obstinacy, its blindness, and you would have shuddered, too, at the thought of those over whom that proud spirit hovers and reigns supreme. In the presence of such immensity, in the presence of the unbounded pride of the dominating spirit, and of the triumphant finality of the world created by that spirit, the hungry soul often quails, yields and submits, seeks its salvation in gin and debauchery and succumbs to a belief in the rightness of the existing order. Reality oppresses, the masses become insensitive and acquire oriental passivity, while the more sceptical among them curse their fate and gloomily look for salvation to Mormonism and such like. And in London the masses can be seen on a scale and in conditions not to be seen anywhere else in the world.

I have been told, for example, that on Saturday nights half a million working men and women and their children spread like the ocean all over town, clustering particularly in certain districts, and celebrate their sabbath all night long until five o'clock in the morning, in other words guzzle and drink like beasts to make up for a whole week. They bring with them their weekly savings, all that was earned by hard work and with many a curse. Great jets of gas burn in meat and food shops, brightly lighting up the streets. It is as if a grand reception were being held for those white negroes. Crowds throng the open taverns and the streets. There they eat and drink. The beer houses are decorated like palaces. Everyone is drunk, but drunk joylessly, gloomily and heavily, and everyone is somehow strangely silent. Only curses and bloody brawls occasionally break that suspicious and oppressively sad silence. . . . Everyone is in a hurry to drink himself into insensibility . . . wives in no way lag behind their husbands and all get drunk together, while children crawl and run about among them.

One such night – it was getting on for two o'clock in the morning – I lost my way and for a long time trudged the streets in the midst of a vast crowd of gloomy people, asking my way almost by gestures, because I do not know a word of English. I found my way, but the impression of what I had seen tormented me for three days afterwards. The populace is much the same anywhere, but there all was so vast, so vivid that you almost physically felt things which up till then you had only imagined. In London you no longer see the populace. Instead, you see a loss of sensibility, systematic, resigned and encouraged. And you feel, as you look at all those social pariahs, that it will be a long time before the prophecy is fulfilled for them, a long time before they are given palm branches and white robes, and that for a long time yet they will continue to appeal to the Throne of the Almighty, crying: 'How long, oh Lord?'[1] And they know it themselves and in the meantime take their revenge on society by producing all kinds of underground mormons, shakers, tramps . . . We are surprised at the stupidity which leads people to become shakers and tramps, and fail to understand that what we have here is a repudiation of our social formula, an obstinate and unconscious repudiation; an instinctive repudiation at any cost, in order to achieve salvation, a horrified and disgusted repudiation of the rest of us. Those millions of people, abandoned and driven away from the feast of humanity, push and crush each other in the

[1]Revelation vi, 10, 11.

47

underground darkness into which they have been cast by their elder brethren, they grope around seeking a door at which to knock and look for an exit lest they be smothered to death in that dark cellar. This is the last desperate attempt to huddle together and form one's own heap, one's own mass and to repudiate everything, the very image of man if need be, only to be oneself, only not to be with us . . .

I saw in London another and similar 'mass', such as you would never see on a like scale anywhere else. An unusual spectacle it certainly was. Anyone who has ever visited London must have been at least once in the Haymarket at night. It is a district in certain streets of which prostitutes swarm by night in their thousands. Streets are lit by jets of gas – something completely unknown in our own country. At every step you come across magnificent public houses, all mirrors and gilt. They serve as meeting places as well as shelters. It is a terrifying experience to find oneself in that crowd. And, what an odd amalgam it is. You will find old women there and beautiful women at the sight of whom you stop in amazement. There are no women in the world as beautiful as the English.

The streets can hardly accommodate the dense, seething crowd. The mob has not enough room on the pavements and swamps the whole street. All this mass of humanity craves for booty and hurls itself at the first comer with shameless cynicism. Glistening, expensive clothes and semi-rags and sharp differences in age – they are all there. A drunken tramp shuffling along in this terrible crowd is jostled by the rich and titled. You hear curses, quarrels, solicitations and the quiet, whispered invitation of some still bashful beauty. And how beautiful they sometimes are with their keepsake faces! I remember once I went into a 'casino'. The music was blaring, people were dancing, a huge crowd was milling round. The place was magnificently decorated. But gloom never forsakes the English even in the midst of gaiety; even when they dance they look serious, not to say sullen, making hardly any steps and then only as if in execution of some duty. Upstairs, in the gallery I saw a girl and stopped in amazement. She was sitting at a little table together with an apparently rich and respectable young man who, by all the signs, was an unaccustomed visitor to the casino. Perhaps he had been looking for her and they had at last found each other and arranged to meet there. He spoke to her little and only in short, jerky phrases as if he was not talking about what really interested him. Their conversation was punctuated by long and frequent silences. She, too, looked sad. Her face was delicate and fine, and there was something deep-hidden and sad, something thoughtful and melancholy in the proud expression of her eyes. I should say she had consumption. Mentally and morally she was, she could not fail to be, above the whole crowd of those wretched women; otherwise, what meaning would there be in a human face? All the same, however, she was then and there drinking gin, paid for by the young man. At last he got up, shook hands with her and went away. He left the casino, while she, her pale cheeks now flushed deep with drink, was soon lost in the crowd of women trading in their bodies.

In the Haymarket I noticed mothers who brought their little daughters to make them ply that same trade. Little girls, aged about twelve, seize you by the arm and beg you to come with them. I remember once amidst the crowd of people in the street I saw a little girl, not older than six, all in rags, dirty, bare-foot and hollow-cheeked; she had been severely beaten, and her body, which showed through the rags, was covered with bruises. She was walking along, as if oblivious of everybody and everything, in no hurry to get anywhere, and Heaven knows why loafing about in that crowd; perhaps she was hungry. Nobody was paying any attention to her. But what struck me most was the look of such distress, such hopeless despair on her face that to see that tiny bit of humanity already bearing the imprint of all that evil and despair was somehow unnatural and terribly painful. She kept on shaking her tousled head as if arguing about something, gesticulated and spread her little hands and then suddenly clasped them together and pressed them to her little bare breast. I went back and gave her sixpence. She took the small silver coin, gave me a wild look full of frightened surprise, and suddenly ran off as fast as her legs could carry her, as if afraid that I should take the money away from her. Jolly scenes, altogether. . . .

And then one night in the midst of a crowd of loose women and debauchees I was stopped by a woman making her way hurriedly through it. She was dressed all in black and her hat almost concealed her face; in fact I had hardly time to make it out, I only remember the steady gaze of her eyes. She said something in broken French which I failed to understand, thrust a piece of paper into my hand and hurried on. I examined the paper at the light of a café window: it was a small square slip. One side bore the words 'Crois-tu cela?' printed on it. The other, also in French: 'I am the Resurrection and the Life' . . ., etc. – the well-known text. This too, you must admit, is rather bizarre. It was explained to me afterwards that that was Catholic propaganda ferreting round everywhere, persistent and tireless. Sometimes they distribute these bits of paper in the streets, sometimes booklets containing extracts from the New Testament and the Bible. They distribute them free, thrust them into people's hands, press them on people. It is ingenious and cunning propaganda. A Catholic priest would search out and insinuate himself into a poor workman's family. He would find, for example, a sick man lying in his rags on a damp floor, surrounded by children crazy from cold and hunger, with a wife famished and often drunk. He would feed them all, provide clothes and warmth for them, give treatment to the sick man, buy medicine for him, become the friend of the family and finally convert them all to the Catholic faith. Sometimes, however, after the sick man has been restored to health, the priest is driven out with curses and kicks. He does not despair and goes off to someone else. He is chucked out again, but puts up with everything and catches someone in the end.

But an Anglican minister would never visit a poor man. The poor are not even allowed inside a church because they have not the money to pay for a seat. More often than not working-class men and women and the poor generally live together in illegitimate union, as marriages are expensive. Many husbands, by the way, beat their wives horribly and disfigure them to the point of death – mostly with the aid of pokers used to break up coal in open grates. They seem to regard them specifically as instruments for beating purposes. At least, in describing family quarrels, injuries and murders, newspapers always mention pokers. The children of the poor, while still very young, often go out into the streets, merge with the crowd and in the end fail to return to their parents.

Anglican ministers and bishops are proud and rich, live in wealthy parishes and dioceses and wax fat with an entirely untroubled conscience. They are great pedants, are highly educated and pompously and seriously believe in their own solidly moral virtues and in their right to preach a staid and complacent morality, to grow fat and to live here for the sake of the rich. It is a religion of the rich, and undisguised at that. At least, this is rational and no one is being deceived. These professors of religion, who carry their convictions to the point of obtuseness, have one amusement, if such it can be called: it is missionary work. They travel all over the earth, penetrate into darkest Africa to convert one savage, and forget the million savages in London because these have nothing to pay them with. But wealthy Englishmen and in fact all the Golden Calves in that country are extremely religious, gloomily, sullenly and peculiarly so. English poets have, from time immemorial, been fond of celebrating the beauty of provincial vicarages, standing in the shade of ancient oaks and elms, their virtuous wives and ideally-beautiful, blond and blue-eyed daughters.

But when night is over and day begins, the same proud and gloomy spirit once again spreads its lordly wings over the gigantic city. It is not worried by what happened during the night, neither is it worried by what it sees all around itself by day. Baal reigns and does not even demand obedience, because he is certain of it. He has boundless faith in himself; contemptuously and calmly and only so as to be left alone, he organizes almsgiving and his self-confidence is not to be shaken. Baal does not close his eyes, as they do in Paris for instance, to certain savage suspicions and alarming facts of life. The poverty, suffering, complaints and torpor of the masses do not worry him in the slightest. Contemptuously, he allows these suspicions and ominous facts to jostle his own life, to sit on his own doorstep for everyone to see. Unlike a Parisian, he does not make strenuous, if cowardly, attempts to convince himself of the falsity of facts, boost his own morale and report to himself that all is quiet and fine. He does not hide his poor, as is done in Paris, lest they disturb and needlessly trouble his sleep. The Parisian likes sticking his head in the sand like an ostrich so as not to see his pursuers catching up with him. In Paris . . . But what am I talking about? I am not in Paris yet! . . . Oh when, my God, will I learn to be orderly? . . .

CHAPTER VI

AN ESSAY ON THE BOURGEOIS

WHY DOES EVERYONE here want to shrink back and shrivel and make out he is only small fry and remain as inconspicuous as is possible: 'I don't exist, I don't exist at all; I am hiding, walk past, please, don't take any notice of me, pretend you don't see me: pass along, pass along!'

'But whom are you talking about? Who shrinks back?'

The bourgeois, of course.

'Come now, he is King, he is everything, *le tiers état c'est tout*, and you say he shrinks back!'

Oh yes, he does; why otherwise, should he have hidden himself behind the Emperor Napoleon?[1] Why has he forgotten the lofty language he used to love so much in the Chamber of Deputies? Why does he not want to remember anything and runs away from any reminders of the past? Why do his thoughts, his eyes, his speech betray so much worry whenever others dare express a wish for something in his presence? Why, whenever he foolishly forgets himself and expresses a wish for something, does he suddenly give a start and begin to deny his own words: 'Good Heavens, what's the matter with me, really!' and for a long time after that he tries scrupulously to make amends for his behaviour by conscientiousness and obedience? Why does he look and almost say: 'Well, now, I'll do a bit of trade in my shop to-day, and, God willing, I'll do a

[1]Napoleon III. *Tr. note.*

53

bit of trade tomorrow too, and perhaps even the day after if the Lord lets me, in His great mercy . . . and then, then – oh, if only I could save just a teeny bit and . . . *après moi le déluge.*' Why does he stick his poor out of the way somewhere and assure people that there aren't any? Why does he make do with official literature? Why does he so much want to convince himself that his newspapers are not open to bribery? Why does he agree to give so much money for the maintenance of police spies? Why does he not dare breathe a word about the Mexican expedition? Why on the stage are husbands made out to be so very noble-minded and rich, while lovers are all so tattered, jobless and friendless, clerks or artists, so much trash? Why does he imagine that all wives without exception are faithful to the last extreme, that the home prospers, that the *pot-au-feu* is cooking on the most virtuous of hearths and that no horns disfigure his forehead? About the horns – this has been decided once and for all, agreed without further ado and taken for granted, and though cabs with drawn blinds constantly ply up and down the boulevards, though time and place can always be found for require- ments of an interesting nature, and though wives very often dress more expensively than could be warranted by the husband's pocket, this has been agreed and ratified, and what more do you want? And why has it been agreed and ratified? The answer is quite obvious: otherwise people might perhaps think that an ideal state of things has not been reached yet, that Paris is not yet Heaven on Earth, that something could perhaps still be wished for, that, therefore, the bourgeois himself is not quite satisfied with the state of things which he supports and which he tries to force on everyone, that the cloth of society has rents which must be mended. This is precisely why the bourgeois smears holes in his shoes with ink lest, God forbid, people should notice anything! The wives, in the meantime, suck sweets, wear gloves of a kind to send

Russian ladies in far-off St Petersburg into envious hysterics, show their little feet and lift their skirts on boulevards with all the grace in the world. What more is needed for perfect bliss? It follows that, circumstances being what they are, novels can no longer bear titles such as, for example, *Wife, Husband and Lover*, because there are no, and cannot be any, lovers. And even if in Paris they were as numerous as the sands of the sea (and maybe they are even more numerous there), there are none there all the same, and there cannot be any because it is thus agreed and ratified and because virtue shines everywhere. That is the way it should be: virtue must shine everywhere. The sight of the great courtyard of the Palais Royal in the evening and up to eleven o'clock at night is surely enough to make anyone shed a sentimental tear. Innumerable husbands stroll about arm-in-arm with their innumerable spouses, their sweet and well-behaved children gambol round them, a little fountain tinkles and its monotonous splash reminds you of something still and quiet, everlasting, permanent, Heidelbergian. And it isn't as if there was only one little fountain in Paris tinkling in this way; there are many little fountains, and everywhere it is the same and one's heart rejoices at the sight of it all.

Paris has an unquenchable thirst for virtue. Nowadays your Frenchman is a serious and reliable man, often tender-hearted, so that I cannot understand why he is so afraid of something even now, and is afraid of it in spite of all the *gloire militaire* which flourishes in France and which Jacques Bonhomme pays so much for. The Parisian dearly loves to trade, but even as he trades and fleeces you in his shop, he fleeces you not for the sake of profit, as in the old days but in the name of virtue, out of some sacred necessity. To amass a fortune and possess as many things as possible – this has become the Parisian's main moral code, to be equated with religious observance. The same thing happened in the old days too, but now – now it has assumed, so to speak, a sort of sacramental aspect. In the old days some value was attached to other things besides money, so that a man with no money but possessing other qualities could expect some kind of esteem; but now – nothing doing. Now you must make money and acquire as many things as possible and you will then be able to expect at least some sort of esteem, otherwise you cannot expect to have any *self*-esteem, let alone the esteem of other people. The Parisian has a very low opinion of himself if he feels his pockets are empty – and he holds this opinion consciously, and with great conviction.

You are allowed to do amazing things if only you have money. Poor Socrates is nothing but a stupid and obnoxious phrase-monger, and is esteemed, if anywhere, only in the theatre because the bourgeois still likes to show esteem for virtue in the theatre. A strange man, this bourgeois: proclaims openly that the acquisition of money is the supreme virtue and human duty and yet dearly loves to play at supremely noble sentiments. All Frenchmen have an extraordinarily noble appearance. The meanest little Frenchman who would sell you his own father for sixpence and add something into the bargain without so much as being asked for it, has at the same time, indeed at the very moment of selling you his own father, such an impressive bearing that you feel perplexed. Go into a shop to buy something and its least important salesman will crush you, simply crush you, with his astounding nobil-ity. These are the very salesmen who serve as models of the most exquisite refinement for our Mikhailovsky Theatre.[1] You are overwhelmed, you feel you have offended the salesman in some way. You have come, let us say, with the intention of spending ten francs, and yet you

[1]Mikhailovsky Theatre – the reference is to the annual season of French plays given by visiting French actors in the Mikhailovsky Theatre in St Petersburg (now the Maly [i.e. small] Theatre of Opera and Ballet in Leningrad). *Tr. note.*

are received as if you were the Duke of Devonshire. For some reason you at once feel terribly ashamed, and you want to assure people quickly that you are not at all the Duke of Devonshire, but somebody quite ordinary, just a simple traveller, and have come in to make a mere ten francs' worth of purchase. But the young man, who has a most fortunate appearance and an ineffably noble expression and at the sight of whom you are ready to acknowledge yourself a rascal (because he has such a noble expression), begins to spread in front of you goods worth tens of thousands of francs. In a minute he has strewn the whole counter with his wares and when you realize how much the poor man will have to fold and wrap up again after you are gone and that he – this Grandison, this Alcibiades, this Montmorency – will have to do it – after whom? After you who, with your unenviable appearance, your vices and defects, your abominable ten francs have dared come and worry so lordly a creature – when you realize all this, you immediately, on the spot and before you have time to leave the counter, begin willy-nilly to despise yourself to the highest possible degree. You repent and curse your fate for having only a hundred francs in your pocket; you throw them down on the counter with an imploring look asking forgiveness. But the article you have bought for your miserable hundred francs is magnanimously wrapped up for you, you are forgiven all the worry and all the trouble which you have caused in the shop and you hasten to come out and vanish. When you get home you are terribly surprised that you wanted to spend only ten francs and have spent one hundred.

How often, when walking down the boulevards or the Rue Vivienne where so many huge haberdashery stores are situated, I used to say to myself: if only Russian ladies were let loose here and . . . but what follows is best known to the factors and bailiffs of estates in Orlov, Tambov and other provinces. In general, Russians in shops long to show that they have a boundless amount of money. On the other hand, what is one to think of such shameless conduct as that of English women, for example, who not only are left completely unperturbed by the fact that some Adonis or William Tell has piled up goods on his counter and turned the whole shop upside down, but even – oh, horrors! – begin to argue for the sake of some ten francs? But William Tell is no simpleton, either. He will take his revenge all right, and for a scarf worth fifteen hundred francs will rook milady twelve thousand, and do it in a way which will leave her completely satisfied.

But in spite of this, the bourgeois is passionately fond of unutterable high-mindedness. On the stage he must have nothing but people completely disinterested in money. Gustave must shine by the light of high-mindedness alone and the bourgeois sheds tears of tender emotion. Without unutterable highmindedness he will not even sleep quietly. And as to taking twelve thousand francs instead of fifteen hundred, this was his duty: he took it because he was virtuous. To steal is wicked and mean – that's what the galleys are for; the bourgeois is ready to forgive a great deal, but he will not forgive stealing even if you and your children should be dying of starvation. But should you steal for virtue's sake, then, oh then, everything is forgiven unto you. It means you want to *faire fortune* and amass many possessions, i.e. perform a natural and human duty. In other words the legal code very clearly defines stealing for low motives, i.e. for the sake of a piece of bread, and stealing in the name of highest virtue. The latter is completely assured, encouraged and is organized on an extraordinarily sound footing.

Why then – I am back at my old theme again – why then does the bourgeois look nervous and ill at ease? What causes him all this worry? The speechifiers? The phrase-mongers? But he can send them all to hell with one kick of his foot. Arguments of pure reason? But reason has proved bankrupt in face of reality, and besides, the rational people themselves, the philosophers and metaphysicians, are now beginning to teach that there are no arguments of pure reason, that pure reason does not even exist in this world, that abstract logic is not applicable to humanity, that there is such a thing as John's, Peter's or Gustave's reason, but there has never been any pure reason, that it is a baseless fiction of the eighteenth century.

Whom should he fear then? Workers? But workers are all of them capitalists too, in their heart of hearts: their one ideal is to become capitalists and amass as many things as possible; such is their nature. People don't get their nature for nothing. All this requires centuries of growth and upbringing. National characteristics cannot easily be altered: it is not easy to get away from centuries-old habits which have become part of our flesh and blood.

Peasants? But French peasants are capitalists *par excellence*, the obtuse kind of capitalists, i.e. the very best and the most ideally perfect type of capitalist that can possibly be imagined. Communists? or perhaps Socialists? But these fellows have considerably compromised themselves in their day, and in his heart of hearts the bourgeois has a profound contempt for them; and yet, for all his contempt, he is afraid of them. In fact, these are the people he fears. But why should he fear them, really? For did not the Abbé Sieyès in his famous pamphlet predict that the bourgeois would be *everything*? 'What is the *tiers état?* Nothing. What must it be? Everything.' Well, now, things have turned out as he foretold them. Of all the words spoken at the time they were the only ones to have come true; the only ones to have remained. But the bourgeois still refuses to believe, somehow, despite the fact that all that has been said since Sieyès' words has collapsed and burst like a soap bubble.

Indeed, soon after him was proclaimed the principle of *liberté, égalité, fraternité*. Excellent. What is *liberté*? Freedom. What freedom? Equal freedom for all to do anything one wants within the limits of the law. When can a man do anything he wants? When he has a million. Does freedom give everyone a million? No. What is a man without a million? A man without a million is not a man who does anything he wants, but a man with whom anything is done that anyone wants. And what follows? What follows is that besides freedom there is also equality, in fact equality before the law. There is only one thing to be said about this equality before the law – that the way in which it is now applied enables, indeed forces, every Frenchman to consider it as a personal insult.

What then remains of the formula? Fraternity, brotherhood. Now this is a most curious concept and, it must be admitted, constitutes the principal stumbling block in the West. The Western man speaks of brotherhood as of the great moving force of humanity, and does not realize that brotherhood cannot come about if it does not exist in fact. What is to be done? Brotherhood must be created at all costs. But it turns out that brotherhood cannot be created, because it creates itself, is given, exists in nature. It was, however, found to be absent in French and in Western nature generally; what was found to exist instead was the principle of individuality, the principle of isolation, of intensified self-preservation, of self-seeking, of self-determination within one's own personality or self, of contrast between this self, the whole of nature and the rest of humanity; and this contrast was considered as an independent and separate principle completely equal and equivalent in value to all that existed apart from itself.

Now such a contrast could not produce brotherhood. Why? Because within brotherhood, true brotherhood, it is not the individual personality, not the self, that should lay claim to its right of equality in value and importance with all the *rest*, but all this *rest* should *itself* approach the individual, the separate self laying this claim, and should

60

itself without being asked, recognize the individual as its equal in value and rights, i.e. the equal of all else that exists in the world. Nay more, the individual who rebels and makes claims should much rather sacrifice both his personality and the whole of himself to society and not only not claim his rights, but on the contrary, hand them over unconditionally to society. But the Western individual is not used to this kind of procedure: he demands by force, he demands rights, he wants to *go shares*. And, naturally, no brotherhood results. There is, of course, the possibility of regeneration. But such a regeneration takes thousands of years, for ideas of this kind must, first of all, become completely ingrained and assimilated in order to become reality. Well then, you will reply, must one loose one's individuality in order to be happy? Is salvation to be found in the absence of individuality? My reply is no, on the contrary, not only should one not loose one's individuality, but one should, in fact, become an individual to a degree far higher than has occurred in the West. You must understand me: a voluntary, absolutely conscious and completely unforced sacrifice of oneself for the sake of all is, I consider, a sign of the highest development of individual personality, its highest power, highest self-possession and highest freedom of the individual will. Voluntarily to lay down one's life for all, be crucified or burned at the stake for the sake of all is possible only at the point of the highest development of individual personality.

A strongly developed individual personality, completely sure of its right to be a personality and deprived of all fear for itself can, in fact, do nothing else out of its personality, can put it, that is, to no other use than to give away the whole of it to all, in order that others, too, may become personalities just as independent and happy. This is a law of nature; man, normally, tends towards it. Here, however, there is a hair, one very, very thin hair but, if it gets into the machine, all will immediately crack and collapse. It is the following: there must not be in this case the slightest motive of personal gain. For example: I offer myself as a total sacrifice for all; and this is as it should be – I should sacrifice myself wholly and irrevocably, without consideration of gain, not thinking in the least that here I am, sacrificing my entire self to society and in exchange society will offer the whole of itself to me. One must, in fact, make one's sacrifice with the intention of giving away everything, and even wish that nothing be given to you in exchange and that no one should spend anything on you.

Now, how is this to be done? Surely, this is rather like trying not to think of a polar bear. Try and set yourself the problem of not thinking about a polar bear and you will see that the damned animal will be constantly in your thoughts. What can we do then? We can do nothing; *it must be done of itself,* the solution must *exist in nature;* must form an unconscious part of the nature of the whole race, what is needed, in short, is the principle of brotherhood and love – we must love. Man must instinctively and of his own accord be drawn towards brotherhood, fellowship and concord and he must be drawn towards them despite immemorial sufferings of his nation, despite the barbarous brutality and ignorance which have become rooted in the nation, despite age-old slavery and foreign invasions. The need for brotherly fellowship must, in fact, have its being in the nature of man, he must be born with it or else have acquired the habit of it from time immemorial.

What would this brotherhood consist in if expressed in rational and conscious language? In each particular individual, without constraint or gain to himself, saying to society: 'We are strong only when we are all together, therefore take the whole of me if you need me, do not think of me when you pass your laws, do not worry in the slightest, I am handing all my rights over to you, and please dispose of me as you wish. It is the height of happiness for me to sacrifice everything to you and in such a way that you do not suffer any loss in consequence. I shall fade away and merge with the completely uniform mass, only let your brotherhood remain and flourish. . . .' And the brotherhood, on the other hand, must say: 'You are giving us too much. We have no right to refuse what you have to give, since you yourself say that therein consists the whole of your happiness; but what can we do, since we, too, care unceasingly for your happiness? You too, then, must take everything from us. We shall always do all we can that you might have as much personal freedom and as much independence as possible. You need no longer fear any enemies, either men or nature. You have the support of all of us, we all guarantee your safety and have your interests at heart night and day because we are brothers, we are all brothers of yours and there are many of us and we are strong. Therefore, do not worry, be of good cheer, fear nothing and put your trust in us.'

After this, there will be no necessity for sharing things out, they will all share themselves out automatically. Love one another and all these things will be added unto you. What a Utopia this is, really! It is all based on sentiment and on nature, and not on reason. Surely this is humiliating for reason. What do you think? Is this Utopia or not?

But then what can a socialist do if the principle of brotherhood is absent in Western man, who recognizes, on the contrary, the individual and personal principle which always insists on isolation and on demanding rights, sword in hand? Because there is no brotherhood he wants to create it, to build it up. To make jugged hare you must begin by having a hare. But there is no hare, there is, in other words, no nature capable of brotherhood, no nature with a belief in brotherhood or drawn towards brotherhood! In desperation, the socialist begins to make and define the future brotherhood, weighs and measures it, throws out the bait of personal advantage, explains, teaches and tells people how much advantage each person will obtain out of this brotherhood, how much each will gain; he determines the utility and cost of each individual, and works out in advance the balance of this world's blessings: how much each individual deserves them and how much each individual must voluntarily contribute to the community in exchange for them at the cost of his own personality. But how can there possibly be any brotherhood if it is preceded by a distribution of shares and by determining how much each person has earned and what each must do?

However, a formula was proclaimed which said: 'Each for all and all for each'. Nothing better than this could, naturally, be thought up, particularly as the whole formula was lifted in its entirety from a well-known book. But then the brethren began to apply this formula in practice and about six months later brought an action against the founder of the brotherhood, Cabet. The Fourierists have, it is said, spent the last 900,000 francs of their capital, but are still trying to organize a brotherhood. The results are nil. Of course it is very tempting to live according to purely rational, if not brotherly, principles, that is, to live well, when you are guaranteed by everyone and nothing is demanded of you except your consent and your work. But here again there is a curious paradox. A man is offered full security, promised food and drink, and found work, and as against this he is merely required to give up a tiny grain of his personal freedom for the sake of the common good – just a tiny, tiny grain. But man does not want to live on these conditions, he finds even the tiny grain too irksome. He thinks that he is being put in gaol, poor fool, and that he would be better off by himself, because then he would have full freedom. And when he is free he is knocked about and refused work, he starves to death and has no real freedom. But all the same, the strange fellow still prefers his own freedom. Naturally enough, the socialist is simply forced to give him up and tell him that he is a fool, that he is not ready yet, not ripe enough to understand what is good for him; that a dumb little ant, a miserable ant is more intelligent than he is because everything is so lovely in an ant-hill, so well-ordered, no one goes hungry and all are happy, everyone knows what he has to do; in fact man has a long way to go before he can hope to reach the standards of an ant-hill.

In other words, though socialism is possible it is possible anywhere but in France.

And so, in final despair, the socialist proclaims at last: liberté, égalité, fraternité *ou la mort*.[1] Then there is no more to be said, and the bourgeois is completely triumphant.

And if the bourgeois is triumphant it means that Sieyès' formula has come true literally and to the last detail. And so the bourgeois is everything. Why then is he shy and retiring, what does he fear? Everyone has collapsed, none has proved capable of standing up to him. In the old days, at the time of Louis–Philippe for example, the bourgeois was not as shy and timid, and yet he reigned then too. Indeed, he still fought then, sensed that he had an enemy and finally defeated him on the June barricades with the aid of rifle and bayonet. But when the battle was over the bourgeois suddenly realized that he was alone in the world, that there was nothing better than himself, that he was the ideal and that instead of trying as hitherto to convince the whole of humanity that he was the ideal, all that was left for him to do was simply to pose with quiet dignity in the eyes of humanity as the last word in human beauty and perfection. A ticklish situation, say what you will. Salvation came from Napoleon III. For the bourgeois he was the gift of the gods, the only way out of the

[1]Based on the slogan proclaimed by Gracchus Babeuf (1760–97). Some of the 'decrees' he published for the benefit of his future communist republic bore the words: 'Egalité, Liberté, Bonheur Commun ou la mort'. *Tr. note.*

difficulty, the only possibility available at the time. From that moment on the bourgeois begins to prosper, pays a frightful lot for his prosperity and fears everything just because he has attained everything. When one attains everything it is hard to *loose* everything. Whence follows, my friends, that he who fears most prospers most. Don't laugh please. For what is a bourgeois these days?

Chapter VII

CONTINUATION OF THE PRECEDING

AND WHY ARE there so many flunkeys among the bourgeois, and of such noble appearance at that? Please don't blame me and don't exclaim that I am exaggerating or being libellous or spiteful. What or whom is my spite directed against? Why should I be spiteful? The fact is simply that there are many flunkeys. Servility seeps increasingly into the very nature of the bourgeois and is increasingly taken for virtue. And that's how it should be in present circumstances. It is their natural consequence. But the main thing, ah, the main thing is that nature itself lends a hand. It isn't only that the bourgeois has a strong, innate propensity for spying, for instance. I am, in fact, convinced that the extraordinary development of police spying in France — and not just ordinary spying, but spying which is both a skill and a vocation, an art in itself — is due to their innate servility in that country. What ideally-noble Gustave, provided only he has not yet accumulated any possessions, will not immediately hand over his lady-love's letters in exchange for ten thousand francs and will not betray his mistress to her husband? Maybe I am exaggerating, but perhaps my words have a certain basis in fact. The Frenchman loves attracting the attention of authority in order to suck up to it, and he does it in a completely disinterested sort of way, with no thought of an immediate reward; he does it on credit, on account. Think, for example of all those job-seekers every time there was a change of regime, formerly so frequent in France. Think of all the tricks they were up to and to which they themselves admitted. Think of one of Barbier's iambics on that score. I remember in a café once, looking at a newspaper dated 3 July. It had, I noticed, an article by a correspondent in Vichy. The Emperor was then staying in Vichy; and so was the Court, of course; there were riding parties, pleasure trips. The correspondent was describing all this. He begins thus: 'We have many excellent horsemen. You have, naturally, guessed who is the most brilliant of them all. His Majesty rides out every day attended by his retinue, etc.'

It's understandable, let them admire their Emperor's brilliant qualities. It is possible to have the greatest respect for his intelligence, his circumspection, his high qualities and so forth. You cannot tell such an enthusiastic gentleman to his face that he is a dissembler.

His reply to you would be: 'Such is my conviction – and that's that' – precisely the reply you would get from some of our own journalists. You see, he is quite safe: he has an answer with which to shut your mouth. The freedom of conscience and of conviction is the first and principal freedom. But in this case what reply can he give you? In this case he no longer pays any regard to the laws of reality, he defies probability and does so intentionally. And why, after all, should he do so intentionally? Surely no one will believe him? The horseman himself is not likely to read it, and even if he does, are the little Frenchman who wrote the *correspondence*, the newspaper which published it and the newspaper's editorial board really all too stupid to grasp that their lord and master has not the slightest use for the reputation of being the first horseman of France, that he does not even expect this reputation in his old age and will naturally refuse to believe it if people try to convince him that he is the most expert rider in all France: they say he is an exceptionally intelligent man. Oh no, there is something else in view here: it may be improbable and ridiculous, the sovereign himself may regard it with disgust and may laugh it to scorn; maybe, maybe, but then he will also see the blind obedience, he will see the infinite obsequiousness, servile, stupid and unreal, but obsequiousness all the same, and that is the main thing. Think it out for yourselves now: if this were not in the spirit of the nation, if such vulgar flattery were not considered entirely possible and ordinary, entirely natural and decent even, could such an article be published in a Paris newspaper? Where in print will you find such flattery except in France? The reason why I speak of the spirit of the nation is precisely because it is not one paper only that writes in this way, but almost all of them, they are all exactly the same, except two or three which are quite independent.

I remember once sitting in a hotel dining room – not in France that time, in Italy, but there was a number of Frenchmen at my table. At that time everyone was always talking of Garibaldi. This was about a fortnight before Aspromonte. Naturally people spoke somewhat enigmatically: some kept silent not wishing to make their meaning absolutely clear, others shook their heads. The general sense of the conversation was that Garibaldi had started a risky, indeed a rash, venture; but this opinion was never stated quite explicitly, because Garibaldi is a man of such different stature to other people that what could in the ordinary way be considered rash might well in his case prove to be reasonable. Gradually the discussion turned to the actual personality of Garibaldi. His qualities were enumerated and the final judgment was rather favourable for the Italian hero.

'Now, there is just one quality in him that amazes me,' exclaimed a Frenchman loudly. He was a pleasant, impressive-looking man, aged about thirty and with that extraordinary nobility of expression in his face which verges on the impudent and which strikes you in all Frenchmen. 'There is just one fact about him which amazes me most of all.'

Everyone, of course, turned to the speaker, their curiosity aroused by his statement.

The quality discovered in Garibaldi was intended to interest everyone.

'For a short time in 1860 he enjoyed unlimited and completely uncontrolled power in Naples. In his hands he held the sum of twenty million francs of public money. He was accountable to no one for that sum. He could have appropriated for himself any amount of it and no one would have held him responsible. He appropriated nothing and handed it all back to the government to the last sou. This is almost incredible!!'

Even his eyes sparkled when he spoke of the twenty million francs.

You can, of course, say what you will about Garibaldi; but to put Garibaldi's name side by side with common embezzlers of public funds – that, obviously, only a Frenchman can do.

And how naïvely, how sincerely he said it! Everything, of course, may be forgiven for the sake of sincerity, even the loss of the capacity to understand and of the feeling for genuinely honourable behaviour; but as I glanced at the face which lit up at the mention of the twenty million francs, the thought quite involuntarily came into my head:

'And what if you, my dear fellow, had held some public office at the time, in place of Garibaldi?'

You will tell me that this, again, is untrue, that all these are individual cases, that precisely the same sort of thing happens in our own country and that I cannot really speak of all Frenchmen. Quite, but I am not, in fact, speaking of all of them. Unutterable nobility of character exists everywhere, while maybe much worse things have occurred in our country. But why, why should this sort of thing be raised up into a virtue? You know what? One can even be despicable in one's moral standards, but not loose one's sense of honour; and in France honest people are very numerous, but they have completely lost their sense of honour, and therefore behave despicably and know not what they do to virtue. The former is, of course, more vicious, but the latter, say what you will, is more contemptible. Such an attitude to virtue bodes no good for the life of a nation. And as to individual cases, I don't want to argue with you. Even a whole nation consists of nothing but individual cases, does it not?

I even thought as follows: perhaps I was mistaken in saying that the bourgeois tries to shrink back and is still constantly afraid of something. He does shrink back, that is true enough, and he is nervous, but taking it all in all, the bourgeois thrives and prospers. Though he tries to deceive himself and though he constantly tells himself that everything is all right, this does not interfere with his outward self-confidence. Not only that, but even inwardly he is self-confident when he gets going. How all this can exist together within him is indeed a problem, but in fact it does. In general, the bourgeois is very far from being stupid, but his intelligence is a short-term one somehow, and works by snatches. He has a great many ready-made concepts stored up, like fuel for the winter, and he seriously intends to live with them for a thousand years, if necessary. However, why mention a thousand years? The bourgeois rarely talks in terms of a thousand years, except, perhaps, when he waxes eloquent. *'Après moi le déluge'* is far more often used and more frequently applied in practice.

And what indifference to everything, what short-lived, empty interests! I had occasion in Paris to visit some people whose house had in my day a constant stream of visitors. They seemed to be afraid of beginning a conversation about anything unusual, anything which was

not petty, any subjects of general interest, you know –
social and political problems or something. It could not, in
this case, it seems to me, be fear of spies, it was simply that
people no longer knew how to think or how to speak
about more serious subjects.

There were people among them, however, who were
terribly interested to know what impression Paris had
made on me, how awe-struck I had been, how amazed,
crushed, annihilated. The Frenchman still thinks himself
capable of morally crushing and annihilating. This, too, is
rather an amusing symptom. I remember particularly one
very charming, very polite, very kind old man to whom I
took a sincere liking. He kept his eyes glued on my face as
he questioned me on my opinion of Paris, and was terribly
hurt whenever I failed to express any particular enthusiasm. His kind face even reflected suffering – literally
suffering, I am not exaggerating. Oh, dear Monsieur Le
M—re! One can never convince a Frenchman, i.e. a
Parisian (because at bottom all Frenchmen are Parisians)
that he is not the greatest man in the whole wide world. As
a matter of fact, he knows very little about the wide
world, apart from Paris, and does not want to know,
either. That's his national trait and a very characteristic one
at that.

But the Frenchman's most characteristic trait is elou-
ence. Nothing can extinguish his love of eloquence which
increases more and more as the years go by. I should
terribly much like to know when precisely this love of
eloquence began in France. Naturally, it started mainly at
the time of Louis XIV. It is a remarkable fact – it is indeed
– that everything in France started at the time of Louis
XIV. But the most remarkable thing is that in the whole of
Europe, too, everything started at the time of Louis XIV.
And what is it he had, that king – I cannot understand! For
he was not really particularly superior to any of the other,
previous, kings. Except, perhaps, that he was the first to

say – *l'état c'est moi*. This had a great success and resounded all over Europe at the time. I imagine it was just that quip that made him famous. It became known surprisingly quickly even in Russia.

A very nationally minded sovereign was this Louis XIV, entirely in the French tradition, and I therefore fail to understand why the French got so out of hand . . . at the end of the last century, I mean. They had their fun and games and went back to the old tradition; that is the way things are shaping; but eloquence, eloquence, oh – it is a stumbling block for a Parisian. He is ready to forget the past entirely, the whole of it, ready to engage in the most sensible conversations and be a most obedient and diligent little boy, but eloquence, eloquence alone he cannot forget even yet. He pines and sighs after eloquence; recalls Thiers, Guizot, Odilon Barrot. 'Ah,' he murmurs to himself sometimes, 'what eloquence there was then!' and begins to think. Napoleon III realized this, came at once to the conclusion that Jacques Bonhomme must not think and little by little brought back eloquence. Six Liberal deputies are kept for this purpose in the Legislative Assembly, six permanent, immutable, real Liberal deputies of the kind, I mean, that probably could not be bribed if one tried. But all the same there are only six of them – there were six, there are six, and six there always will be. You needn't worry, there will never be more, but there will never be any less, either. It looks very cunning at first sight. In practice, however, it is quite simple and is done by means of the *suffrage universel*. Naturally, all appropriate measures are taken to prevent them talking too much. but they are allowed to chatter.

Every year at the requisite time the most important state problems are discussed and the Parisian is blissfully thrilled. He knows there will be eloquence and is pleased. Naturally he knows very well that there will be nothing but eloquence, that there will be words, words, words and that these words will lead to absolutely nothing. But this, too, pleases him very, very much indeed. And he is the first to find it all extremely sensible. The speeches of some of these six deputies are particularly popular. And a deputy is always ready to make speeches for the sake of public entertainment. Oddly enough he is quite sure himself that his speeches will lead to nothing, and that the whole thing is but a joke, an innocent game, a masquerade and nothing else, and yet he speaks, speaks for years on end, speaks excellently, and even takes great pleasure in it. And all the other members who listen to him swoon away with delight. 'Wonderful speaker, that man!' – and the President and the whole of France swoon away with delight. The deputy comes to the end of his speech and the tutor of these nice and well-behaved children gets up in his turn. He solemnly declares that the essay on the set subject: 'The Sunrise', has been excellently prepared and developed by the honourable member. 'We have,' he says, 'admired the honourable speaker's talent, his ideas and the admirable conduct these ideas reveal, he has given us all, all, a great deal of pleasure . . . However, although the honourable member has fully deserved his prize – a book bearing the inscription 'For Good Conduct and Progress in Study' – in spite of this, I say, for reasons of a higher order, the honourable member's speech will not do at all. I hope the right honourable members will agree with me.' At this point he turns to all the deputies and gives them a stern glance. The deputies, still swooning with delight, immediately break into frantic applause at the tutor's words, yet at the same time with touching enthusiasm, they grasp the Liberal deputy's hands and thank him then and there for the pleasure he has given them and beg him to give them this Liberal pleasure again next time, with the tutor's permission. The tutor graciously permits; the author of 'The Sunrise' departs, proud of his success; the deputies go back, smacking their lips, to the bosom of their families, and in the evening, give vent to their delight by walking about in the Palais-Royal arm-in-arm with their spouses and listening to the splash of little fountains, while the tutor, after submitting a full report to the Authority concerned, declares to the whole of France that everything is all right.

Sometimes, however, when some more important business is in hand the stakes for which the game is played are higher, more important too. Prince Napoleon himself is brought to one of the Assembly's sittings. Prince Napoleon suddenly begins to act the part of the Opposition and quite frightens all these young pupils. A solemn hush descends upon the classroom. Prince Napoleon plays the Liberal, the Prince does not agree with the Government, he considers that such and such measures should be adopted. The Prince censures the Government, in other words things are being said which (it is assumed) these very same nice children could say if only their tutor were to leave the classroom for one minute. Within reason, of course, even so; besides, the assumption is absurd because all these nice children are so nicely brought up that they would not so much as budge even if the tutor left them for a whole week. And so when Prince Napoleon's speech is over, the tutor gets up and solemnly declares that the essay on the set subject: 'The Sunrise', has been excellently prepared and developed by the honourable speaker. 'We have admired the talent, the eloquently expressed ideas and the virtue of the gracious Prince . . . We are quite prepared to let him have a prize for diligence and progress in his studies, but . . .' and so forth, in other words all the things that have been said before. Naturally, the entire form is delighted and breaks into frantic applause, the Prince is taken back home, the virtuous pupils disperse and leave the classroom like the virtuous little goody-goodies they are, and in the evening go out for a walk in the Palais–Royal together with their spouses and listen to the pleasant splash of little fountains, etc., etc., etc. In short, order reigns supreme.

We lost our way once in the *salle des pas perdus* and instead of a criminal court we stumbled into a court dealing with civil cases.

A curly-haired lawyer in cap and gown was making a speech, scattering pearls of eloquence. The presiding judge, the other judges, the lawyers and the public wallowed in all this with obvious delight. The hush was awe-inspiring; we tip-toed in. The case dealt with a legacy; some monks were mixed up in the case. Monks are now constantly mixed up in legal proceedings, mainly dealing with legacies. The most disgraceful, the most scandalous occurrences are now being brought out into the light of day; but the public keeps silent and is very little scandalized, because monks wield considerable power now, and the bourgeois is very docile. The holy fathers are becoming increasingly convinced of the superiority of a bit of capital over all else, over dreams and similar things, increasingly convinced, in fact, that a little money on the side brings power with it. For what's in mere eloquence? Eloquence by itself does not suffice nowadays. But there, I personally think, they are slightly mistaken. Of course, a bit of capital is a twice-blessed thing, but eloquence, too, will get you a long way with a Frenchman. The wives generally fall under the spell of the monks – and much more so now than at any other time in the past. There is every hope too, that the bourgeois will follow suit.

The case revealed how for years on end the holy fathers had worked cunningly and scientifically (they have evolved a science for this sort of thing), bringing moral pressure to bear on a lovely and very wealthy lady, how they had induced her to live in a convent, and how they had terrorized her there till she became ill and hysterical, and how they had done it all in a calculated and scientifically graduated way. Finally, having made a sick woman of her and reduced her to imbecility, they persuaded her that to see relatives was a great sin in the sight of the Lord, and little by little they succeeded in keeping away all her relations. 'Even her fifteen-year-old niece with a soul as virgin-pure as a new-born babe's, an angel of purity and innocence, even she dared not enter the cell of her adored aunt, who loved her beyond all else and who, as a result of crafty machinations, could no longer take her in her arms and give her a kiss on her *front virginal*, where the white angel of innocence had his seat' . . . And so on in the same strain; it was wonderful. The lawyer making the speech was obviously melting with joy at the thought of being able to speak so well, the President of the court was melting too, and so was the public. The holy fathers lost their battle solely on account of this eloquence. But this does not dishearten them, of course; for each battle lost they win fifteen.

'Who is the lawyer?' I asked a young student, who was one of the most fervent listeners. There were many students there and all of them so quiet and well-mannered. He looked at me with surprise.

'Jules Favre,' he replied at last, with such contemptuous pity that I naturally felt abashed. Thus I had the chance to get to know the very flower of French eloquence at its main source, as you might say.

But there is a vast number of these sources. The bourgeois is riddled with eloquence. We went once to the Pantheon to have to look at the great men. It was the wrong time to come at and we had to pay two francs. Thereupon a venerable, if decrepit, disabled soldier took the keys and led us to the church crypt. On the way there he still spoke like a man, even though the absence of teeth made him mumble a little. But as soon as we were down in the crypt and he had brought us to the first tomb, he broke into sing-song.

'*Ci-gît* Voltaire, Voltaire this great genius of lovely

France. He abolished prejudice, overcame ignorance, wrestled with the angel of darkness and held high the torch of enlightenment. He reached greatness in his tragedies, though France already had Corneille.'

He was clearly repeating a lesson he had learnt and committed to memory. Someone had once written out the whole sermon for him on a piece of paper and he got it off by heart for the rest of his life: pleasure shone on his kind old face as he began perorating in high-falutin' style for our benefit.

'*Ci-gît* Jean-Jacques Rousseau,' he continued at the next tomb. 'Jean-Jacques, *l'homme de la nature et de la vérité!*'

Suddenly I wanted to laugh. A high-falutin' style can make anything appear ridiculous. Besides, it was obvious that even as he spoke of *nature* and *vérité* the poor old man had no idea what he was talking about.

'How odd!' I said to him. 'Of these two great men one spent his life calling the other a liar and a wretch, and the other simply called the first a fool. And here they have come together, almost next to each other.'

'Monsieur, monsieur!' began the disabled soldier. He wanted to reply something but didn't and quickly took us to another tomb.

'*Ci-gît* Lannes, Marshal Lannes' – he went off into his sing-song again – 'one of the greatest heroes France, so rich in heroes, has ever had. He was not only a great marshal and the most skilful leader of troops apart from the great Emperor, but he enjoyed an even greater happiness. He was the friend . . .'

'Of course,' I said, eager to shorten the speech, 'he was the friend of Napoleon.'

'Monsieur,' interrupted the disabled soldier, 'let me speak.' He sounded somewhat hurt.

'Go on then, I am listening.'

'But he enjoyed an even greater happiness. He was the friend of the great Emperor. Not one of all his other marshals had had the happiness of becoming the great man's friend. Marshal Lannes alone proved worthy of that great honour. As he lay dying for his country on the field of battle . . .'

'Well, yes, he had both his legs torn off by a cannon ball.'

'Monsieur, monsieur,' exclaimed the soldier almost in tears, 'do let me speak myself. You know it all perhaps . . . But let me tell it too.'

The strange fellow was terribly keen to tell the story himself, even though we knew it all before.

'As he lay dying for his country,' he began once more, 'on the field of battle, the Emperor, struck to the heart and mourning his great loss . . .'

'Came to say farewell to him,' said I, unable to restrain myself from interrupting him again. But I immediately felt I should not have done it and was overcome by remorse.

'Monsieur, monsieur,' said the old man dolefully and reproachfully looking at me straight in the eye and shaking his grey head. 'Monsieur, I know, I am sure you know all this better than I do, perhaps. But you have yourself taken me on to show you: let me speak then. There's not much left now . . . Then the Emperor, struck to the heart and mourning (alas, in vain!) the great loss which he, the army and the whole of France had sustained, approached the deathbed and by his last farewell soothed the cruel sufferings of the great captain who died almost in his presence – C'est fini, monsieur,' he added, casting a reproachful glance at me; and continued on his way.

'And here is another tomb; and those over there . . . quelques sénateurs,' he added with complete indifference and gave a casual nod in the direction of several other tombs nearby. He had exhausted the whole of his eloquence on Voltaire, Jean-Jacques and Marshal Lannes.

This was a direct example, coming from the people so

to speak, of the love of eloquence. Is it possible that all the speeches held in the National Assembly, the Convention, and the Clubs in which the nation had almost directly participated and in which it had been re-educated, is it possible, I repeat, that they have left only one trace: the love of eloquence for the sake of eloquence?

Chapter VIII

BRIBRI AND MA BICHE

AND WHAT ABOUT spouses? Spouses thrive and flourish. By the way, why you may ask, do I write 'spouses' instead of wives? Lofty style, my dear sirs, that's why. The bourgeois, whenever he has recourse to lofty style, always says 'mon épouse'. And though other classes simply say *ma femme* – my wife – like everywhere else, it is better to follow the national spirit of the majority and use the lofty style of speech. It's more characteristic. Besides, there are other names as well. When the bourgeois is in a sentimental mood or wants to be unfaithful to his wife he always calls her *ma biche* – my doe. And conversely a loving wife in an access of dainty skittishness calls her darling bourgeois *bribri*, to the great delight of the bourgeois.

Bribri and Ma Biche always thrive but now more than ever. It is, of course, understood (tacitly, almost) that Ma Biche and Bribri must in our troubled times, serve as models of society's virtue, harmony and blissful state, and as a reproach to the odious nonsense of absurd communist tramps; but apart from that, Bribri becomes, maritally speaking, increasingly amenable every year. He understands that his Biche cannot be kept back, whatever is done or said, that a Parisienne is made to have a lover, and that a husband cannot avoid a couple of horns. He will naturally keep mum while his savings are still meagre and his possessions few. However, as soon as he has both,

Bribri becomes more exacting in every way, because he then acquires a great respect for himself. He begins to consider Gustave in a different light too, particularly if the latter is no more than a ragamuffin and has but few possessions.

In general, a Parisian who has a little money and wants to get married chooses a wife who also has a little money. Not only that, but they go through each other's accounts first, and if they discover that francs and possessions are equal on either side, they unite. This happens everywhere else too; but here the law of the equality of pockets has developed into a peculiar custom. For instance, if a girl has so much as a penny more than a would-be suitor she will never be allowed to marry him and a better Bribri is then looked for. Besides, love-matches are becoming increasingly impossible and are regarded as almost indecent. The reasonable custom which invariably demands the equality of pockets and the marriage of fortunes is very rarely broken – more rarely, I should think, than anywhere else. The bourgeois has organized his wife's money excellently well to his own advantage. That is precisely why he is often ready to close his eyes to his Biche's escapades and not to notice a number of annoying things, for otherwise, in case of disagreement between them, the question of the dowry can raise its ugly head. Besides, should his Biche ever take to following fashion beyond her means, Bribri would take note but voice no objection; his wife might ask less for her dresses. Ma Biche is then much easier to deal with. Anyway, as marriages are for the most part marriages of fortunes and very little attention is paid to mutual affection, Bribri himself is not averse to letting his glances stray away from his own Biche. Thus, it is best not to interfere with each other. In this way more harmony reigns in the home, and the beloved names – Bribri and Ma Biche – are ever more frequently murmured by the loving couples.

As a matter of fact, to be quite frank, Bribri has even here succeeded in securing his own position. The police officer is always at his disposal. Such is the law of which he is himself the author. If the worst comes to the worst and he finds the pair of lovers *en flagrant délit*, he can even kill them, without having to answer for his actions. Ma Biche knows this and approves it.

A long period of protection and guardianship has reduced Ma Biche to such a state of mind that she neither complains nor dreams, as in certain other barbarous and ridiculous countries, of, for instance, receiving a university education, joining clubs and becoming a Member of Parliament. She prefers to lead her present ethereal and, so to speak, canary-like existence. She is decked out in fine clothes and gloves and taken for drives, she dances, she sucks sweets, superficially she is received like a queen and superficially, men are at her feet. This form of relationship has been worked out with a surprisingly high degree of success and decorum. In short, the rules of chivalry are observed, and what more can she want? She will not be deprived of Gustave. Neither does she want her life to have a virtuous and noble purpose, etc. She is really quite as much of a capitalist and quite as niggardly as her husband. When the canary years are over, when, that is, Ma Biche can no longer dupe herself about being a canary, when the possibility of a new Gustave becomes an absolute absurdity to even the most fervent and self-satisfied imagination, she suddenly undergoes a rapid and unpleasant transformation. Gone are daintiness, finery, skittishness. For the most part she becomes a bad-tempered housewife and a church mouse, who helps her husband to hoard his pennies. A sort of cynicism suddenly takes hold of her; lassitude, spite, coarse instincts, point-less life, cynical talk – all suddenly make their appearance. Some even become slatternly. Of course, this is not always the case, there are other more cheering phenomena too;

similar social relationships can also be observed elsewhere – of course – but . . . in France all this is more natural, more genuine, more spontaneous, fuller, it is all more national. Here is the source and embryo of that bourgeois form of society which now reigns throughout the world, in general imitation of the great nation.

Certainly Ma Biche is queen – superficially. It is difficult to imagine the exquisite politeness with which she is surrounded, the importunate attention which is paid to her everywhere in society as well as in the streets. The refinement of it is amazing, but it is sometimes so mawkish that for any honest soul it would be unbearable. The obvious sham of it would cut him to the quick. But Ma Biche is herself a great rogue and . . . that is all she wants . . . she will always get her way and will always prefer devious means to the honest and straightforward: the results, she thinks, are more certain and she gets more fun. And for Ma Biche intrigue and fun is everything; it's the whole point. But then, look at the way she is dressed, at the way she walks along the streets. Ma Biche is simpering, affected, unnatural through and through, but this is precisely what captivates people, especially those who are blasé or partly depraved and who have lost all taste for fresh and natural beauty. Ma Biche has a very under-developed personality; she has a bird's brain and heart, but on the other hand she is dainty, she has the secret of innumerable little tricks and shifts which subjugate you and make you follow her as a piquant novelty. But in fact she is rarely beautiful. There is something evil in her face, even. But it does not matter, the face is mobile and cheerful and possesses to the highest degree the secret of counterfeiting feeling and nature. Maybe what you like about her is not that she achieves the natural by means of the counterfeit, but you are fascinated by the actual process of achievement by counterfeit, the art of it fascinates you.

The Parisian for the most part does not care whether it is

true love or a good counterfeit. He perhaps even prefers the counterfeit. A kind of Eastern view of women is gaining currency in Paris. The camelia is more and more in fashion. 'Take the money and dupe me as well as you can – give me a counterfeit imitation of love, in other words': that's what is required of a camelia. Very little more is required of a wife, at least that is all that's asked of her, and there is, therefore, tacit indulgence for Gustave. Besides, the bourgeois knows that in her old age his Biche will enter fully into his interests and show a great deal of zeal in helping him to amass his fortune. She helps him a lot even in her youth. She sometimes carries on the whole trade, lures in the customers and is, in fact, his right hand, his chief clerk. And in the circumstances, he naturally forgives her her Gustave.

In the streets woman enjoys inviolability. No one will offend her and she is always given the right of way. Whereas in Russia any woman who is not quite old cannot make a step in the streets without someone – some soldier or debauchee – peering under her hat and trying to effect an introduction.

However, in spite of the possibility of Gustave, the ordinary, ritual form of relationship between Bribri and his Biche is quite charming and frequently naïve. In general almost all foreigners are incomparably more naïve than the Russians. This struck me immediately. It is difficult to explain this precisely – it is a thing that must be noted for oneself. *Le russe est sceptique et moqueur*, say the French about us, and this is, in fact, so. We are greater cynics and appreciate our national patrimony less, do not like it even, anyway have not the highest respect for it and do not understand it; we meddle in European affairs and take the whole of humanity as our field without ourselves belonging to any nation, and, therefore, naturally adopt a much cooler attitude to everything, rather as if we were performing a duty – and we are certainly more detached.

But I am digressing. Bribri is sometimes very naïve. When walking round the little fountains, for instance, he will start explaining to his Biche the reason for the fountain's upward jet; he explains to her the laws of nature, parades to her face his national pride in the beauty of the Bois de Boulogne, flood-lighting, the play of the *grandes eaux* in Versailles, the triumphs of the Emperor Napoleon and the *gloire militaire*; he takes delight in her curiosity and pleasure and is himself very pleased.

The most rascally Biche is also fairly tender to her spouse, and her tenderness is real and not counterfeit, in spite of the husband's horns. I do not pretend, of course, to be able to take roofs off houses, like Le Sage's Devil. I am only telling of things that have struck me, things I have observed. Ma Biche might say to you: '*Mon mari n'a pas encore vu la mer,*' and her voice betrays a sincere and naïve sympathy for him. It means that her husband has not yet been to Brest or Boulogne or somewhere to have a look at the sea.

You must know that the bourgeois has certain very naïve and very serious needs, which have almost become a general bourgeois habit. For example, apart from the need to make money and the need for eloquence, the bourgeois has two other needs, two most legitimate needs, hallowed by general custom and to which he adopts an extremely serious, well-nigh pathetic attitude.

The first is to see the sea – *voir la mer*. The Parisian sometimes lives and works in Paris all his life and does not see the sea. Why should he? All unbeknown to himself he has a strong, a passionate desire for it, puts off the journey from year to year because he is usually retained by business, grieves, and his wife sincerely shares his grief. There is, in general, a great deal of sentimentality in all this, and I have great respect for it. At last he succeeds in finding time and money, gets ready and goes off 'to see the sea' for a few days. On his return, he tells his impressions in rapturous and florid style to his wife, his relations and his friends, and all his life he treasures with delight the memory of having seen the sea.

The bourgeois's other legitimate and equally strong need is to *se rouler dans l'herbe*. The fact is that as soon as a Parisian leaves town, he loves, and even considers it his duty, to lie on the grass for a bit; he does it with dignity and the feeling that he thereby communes *avec la nature*, and is particularly delighted if someone watches him at it. In general, the Parisian out of town considers it his immediate duty to become at once skittish, breezy and even dashing, in fact to appear natural and near *la nature*.

L'homme de la nature et de la vérité! Could it have been Jean-Jacques who first instilled in the bourgeois this intense respect for *la nature*? As a matter of fact, the Parisian allows himself to have these two needs – *voir la mer* and *se rouler dans l'herbe* – for the most part only after he has acquired a certain amount of wealth, in short only after he has gained respect for himself, is proud of himself and regards himself as a human being. *Se rouler dans l'herbe* can be ten, twenty times sweeter when it takes place on one's own land, bought for money earned by one's own toil. Generally speaking, on retirement the bourgeois likes to buy a piece of land somewhere, acquire a house, a garden, his own fence, his own hens, his own cow. It matters not if it is all on a microscopic scale – the bourgeois is childishly, touchingly delighted: '*mon arbre, mon mur,*' he constantly repeats to himself and to all his guests and never thereafter ceases from repeating it to himself throughout his life. That is when it becomes sweeter than ever to *se rouler dans l'herbe*. To perform this duty, he will always have a lawn in front of his house. Someone once told me of a bourgeois who could not get grass to grow on the spot intended for the lawn. He tried to grow it, watered it, put down turf brought from elsewhere – but the soil was sandy and he had no success, nothing took. It was just his luck to have that type of soil in front of his house. Then, it seems, he bought himself artificial lawn grass; went to Paris specially for it, brought back a round piece of turf, about two yards in diameter, and used to spread it out every afternoon in order to satisfy his legitimate need of lying on the grass even at the cost of self-deception. At the first flush of delight at the acquisition of property a bourgeois is probably quite capable of doing this, so that there is nothing inherently improbable about it.

But let me say a couple of words about Gustave. Gustave is, of course, similar to the bourgeois, i.e. he is a clerk, a tradesman, a civil servant, *homme de lettres*, officer. Gustave is the same Bribri only not married. But that does not matter, what matters is what Gustave now pretends to be, what he masquerades as, his present appearance and disguise. The ideal Gustave changes with the times and is always represented in the theatre in the aspect in which he is familiar to society. The bourgeois is particularly fond of the variety theatre, but he is even fonder of melodrama. The humble, the gay variety theatre is the only form of art which it is almost impossible to transplant to another soil; it can live only in the place of its birth, which is Paris. The bourgeois is fascinated by it, but it does not fully satisfy him. He cannot help considering it a mere trifle. He wants the sublime, he wants the utterly high-minded, he wants sentiment; and melodrama contains all this. The Parisian cannot live without melodrama. Melodrama will not die so long as the bourgeois lives.

It is interesting to note that variety theatre, too, is now gradually changing. It is still gay and screamingly funny as it has always been, but nowadays a new element is creeping in – that of moral preaching. The bourgeois loves lecturing both himself and his Biche, and considers it his essential, indeed his sacred, duty to do so at every turn.

Besides, the bourgeois now rules autocratically; he is a

force; and the little scribblers who write variety and melodrama are always flunkeys and always flatter force. That is why the bourgeois now always triumphs even when held up to ridicule, and in the end he is always told that everything is all right. Presumably, this information completely reassures the bourgeois. Every faint-hearted person who is not certain of success in whatever he undertakes, feels an acute need for self-delusion, self-encouragement and self-comfort. He even begins to believe in happy auguries. This is precisely what happens here. But melodrama presents lofty characters and lofty models; it has no humour – instead, you have a deeply moving triumph of all Bribri loves and admires so much. What he likes most is public peace and the right to save money in order to have an assured home. That is the spirit in which melodramas are now written. And that is the spirit in which Gustave is now presented. Gustave is always the true measure of what at any moment the bourgeois considers to be the ideal of unutterable high-mindedness.

Formerly, a long time ago, Gustave was supposed to be a kind of poet, artist, unrecognized and downtrodden genius suffering persecution and injustice. He put up a praiseworthy struggle and the whole thing always ended with the *Vicomtesse*, who was secretly in love with him, and whom he treated with contemptuous indifference, uniting him with her ward Cécile, who never had a penny before, but who was suddenly discovered to have an immense amount of money. As a rule, Gustave revolted against this and spurned the money. But then his work was crowned with success at an exhibition. Three funny English lords immediately burst into his flat and offered him a hundred thousand francs each for his next picture. Gustave laughed at them contemptuously and declared in bitter despair that all men were rascals, unworthy of his brush, and that he would not offer up art, sacred art, to the profanation of pygmies who had not noticed till then how great he was. But the Viscountess would burst in and declare that Cécile was dying of love for him and that therefore he should paint pictures. At that point it would dawn on Gustave that the Viscountess, his former enemy, as a result of whose machinations not a single one of his works had ever been accepted for exhibition, is secretly in love with him; and he realizes that she used to try to get her own back on him merely out of jealousy. Naturally, Gustave immediately takes the money from the three lords, after giving them a piece of his mind once again, thus affording them great pleasure, runs off to Cécile, agrees to take her million and forgives the Viscountess who departs to her country house; he duly marries, and settles down to children, a flannel vest, a *bonnet de coton* and evening strolls with his Biche round the lovely little fountains, whose quiet splash reminds him, of course, of the permanence, stability and sereneness of his earthly happiness.

Sometimes it happens that Gustave is not a clerk, but some oppressed and downtrodden orphan who in his heart of hearts nurtures unutterably noble sentiments. Suddenly it is discovered that he is by no means an orphan but the legitimate son of Rothschild. He gets millions. But proudly and contemptuously Gustave spurns these millions. Why? Because eloquence demands it. At this point in bursts Madame Beaupré, who is in love with him, but married to a banker who is his employer. She declares that Cécile is about to die of love for him and that he must go and save her. Gustave guesses that Madame Beaupré is in love with him, swipes the millions and after swearing at everyone in most foul language because humanity has not the likes of him for unutterable high-mindedness, he goes to Cécile and is united with her. The banker's wife departs for her country house, Beaupré is triumphant because his wife, after having hesitated on the brink of perdition, remains pure and undefiled, and Gustave settles down to having children and strolls out in the evening round the lovely little fountains whose splash reminds him etc., etc.

Nowadays unutterable high-mindedness is more often than not represented by an army officer or a sapper or something, mostly in army uniform and inevitably with the ribbon of the Legion of Honour 'bought at the price of his blood'. This ribbon, by the way, is horrible. The bearer of it becomes so conceited that one can hardly meet him, or sit in the same carriage, or next to him in the theatre, or meet him in a restaurant. He almost spits at you, swaggers about shamelessly in front of you, he swaggers so much he snorts and chokes so that you end up by feeling sick, you have a bilious attack and are obliged to send for a doctor. But the French love it.

It is a remarkable fact, too, that on the stage very special attention is now paid to Monsieur Beaupré as well – far more, at least, than formerly. Beaupré has, of course, made a lot of money and acquired very many things. He is simple and straightforward and made a little ridiculous by his bourgeois habits and the fact of being a husband; but he is kind, honest, magnanimous and unutterably high-minded in the act in which he must suffer from the suspicion that his Biche is unfaithful to him. But in spite of everything he magnanimously decides to forgive her. She turns out, of course, to be as pure as a dove: it was all a joke on her part, and though she had been carried away by Gustave, Bribri with his crushing magnanimity is dearer to her than anyone else. Cécile, naturally, is as penniless as ever, but only in the first act; later on it turns out she has a million. Gustave is as proud and contemptuously high-minded as ever, only he swaggers more because he is an officer. The things that are dearest to him in the world are his cross, bought at the price of blood, and *'l'épée de mon père'*. Of his father's sword he talks everywhere, constantly and irrelevantly; you do not even understand what it is all about; he swears and spits, but everyone treats him with respect, while the audience weeps and claps (literally weeps). He is, of course, penniless – this is a *sine qua non*. Madame Beaupré is in love with him, of course; so is Cécile, but he has no inkling of that. Her love makes Cécile grunt and groan throughout the five acts.

At last it begins to snow, or something like that. Cécile wants to throw herself out of the window. But two shots are heard under the window and everyone flocks in; enter slowly Gustave pale and with his hand bandaged. The ribbon bought at the price of blood sparkles on his coat. Cécile's slanderer and seducer has been punished. Gustave at last forgets that Cécile loves him and that it is all Madame Beaupré's tricks. But Madame Beaupré is pale and frightened, and Gustave guesses her love for him. However, another shot is heard. This is Beaupré committing suicide out of despair. Madame Beaupré gives a scream and rushes to the door, but in comes Beaupré himself carrying a fox or something he had just killed. Ma Biche has had her lesson and will never forget it. She clings to Bribri who forgives everything.

But then suddenly Cécile gets a million and Gustave is again in revolt. He does not want to marry. Gustave makes a fuss, Gustave uses bad language. It is quite essential that Gustave should use bad language and spurn a million, otherwise the bourgeois will never forgive him; there would not be enough unutterable high-mindedness. Please do not think that the bourgeois is inconsistent with himself. Don't you worry: the million will not avoid the happy couple, it is inevitable and in the end always appears as a reward of virtue. The bourgeois will never be untrue to himself. In the end Gustave takes the million and Cécile, and then begin the inevitable little fountains, cotton nightcaps, the splash of water, etc., etc. In this way there is a lot of sentiment and unutterable high-mindedness by the sackful, and the triumphant Beaupré, crushing everyone with his family virtues, and, above all, the million which appears like Nemesis, like a law of nature, to which all honour, glory and worship, etc., etc.

Bribri and his Biche leave the theatre completely satisfied, reassured and comforted. Gustave accompanies them and furtively kisses the hand of another man's Biche as he helps her into the cab. All is as it should be.

ALSO PUBLISHED BY QUARTET BOOKS

A Landowner's Morning
Family Happiness
and
The Devil
Three Novellas by
LEO TOLSTOY

Translated and Introduced by
Kyril and April FitzLyon

These three novellas are among the finest and yet, surprisingly, among the least known and most rarely translated
of Tolstoy's works. *A Landowner's Morning* and *Family
Happiness* were written at the beginning of his literary
career, *The Devil* at the end of it. *Family Happiness* – an
ironical title – and *The Devil*, both curiously modern, deal
with marriage and sex, and show Tolstoy's ideas on these
subjects in youth and old age. *A Landowner's Morning*
develops for the first time a theme which was to absorb
Tolstoy throughout his long career: the conflict between
traditional values and material progress.

QUARTET ENCOUNTERS

The purpose of this new paperback series is to bring together influential and outstanding works of twentieth-century European literature in translation. Each title has an introduction by a distinguished contemporary writer, describing a personal or cultural 'encounter' with the text, as well as placing it within its literary and historical perspective.

Quartet Encounters will concentrate on fiction, although the overall emphasis is upon works of enduring literary merit, whether biography, travel, history or politics. The series will also preserve a balance between new and older works, between new translations and reprints of notable existing translations. Quartet Encounters provides a much-needed forum for prose translation, and makes accessible to a wide readership some of the more unjustly neglected classics of modern European literature.

Quartet Books is pleased to announce the first six titles:

Aharon Appelfeld · *The Retreat*

Translated from the Hebrew by Dalya Bilu,
with an introduction by Gabriel Josipovici
'A small masterpiece . . . the vision of a remarkable poet'
New York Times Book Review

Grazia Deledda · *After the Divorce*

Translated from the Italian by Susan Ashe,
with an introduction by Sheila MacLeod
'What [Deledda] does is create the passionate complex
of a primitive populace' D.H. Lawrence

Carlo Emilio Gadda · *That Awful Mess on Via Merulana*

Translated from the Italian by William Weaver,
with an introduction by Italo Calvino
'One of the greatest and most original Italian novels
of our time' Alberto Moravia

Gustav Janouch · *Conversations with Kafka*

Translated from the German by Goronwy Rees,
with an introduction by Hugh Haughton
'I read it and was stunned by the wealth of new material . . .
which plainly and unmistakably bore the stamp of Kafka's
genius' Max Brod

Henry de Montherlant · *The Bachelors*

Translated from the French and with an introduction
by Terence Kilmartin
'One of those carefully framed, precise and acid
studies on a small canvas in which French writers
again and again excel' V.S. Pritchett

Stanislaw Ignacy Witkiewicz · *Insatiability*

Translated from the Polish by Louis Iribarne,
with an introduction by Czeslaw Milosz
'A study of decay: mad, dissonant music; erotic perversion;
. . . and complex psychopathic personalities'
Czeslaw Milosz

FORTHCOMING TITLES

Hermann Broch · *The Sleepwalkers*

'One of the greatest European novels . . .
masterful' Milan Kundera

Pär Lagerkvist · *The Dwarf*

'A considerable imaginative feat'
Times Literary Supplement

Robert Bresson · *Notes on Cinematography*

'Bresson is the French cinema, as . . .
Mozart is German music' Jean-Luc Godard

Rainer Maria Rilke · *Rodin and Selected Prose*

'Rilke's essay remains the outstanding interpretation
of Rodin's oeuvre' William Tucker